AdvancementServices

*Research
and Technology
Support for
Fund Raising*

*Edited by John H. Taylor
Director of Alumni and
Development Records
Duke University*

© 1999 by the Council for Advancement and Support of Education
ISBN 0-89964-349-3
Printed in the United States of America

The Council for Advancement and Support of Education is the largest international association of education institutions, with more than 2,900 colleges, universities, and independent elementary and secondary schools as members.
Representing these institutions are advancement professionals in the disciplines
of alumni relations, communications, and fund raising.

CASE offers high-quality training, information resources, and a wide variety of
books, videotapes, and materials for advancement professionals.

For more information or to place an order, call (800) 554-8536 (US and Canada)
or (301) 604-2068 (International). To receive our catalog, call (202) 328-2273.

Visit CASE online at *www.case.org*.

Book design: Fletcher Design
Editors: Karla Taylor and Nancy Raley
Research: CASE Information Center

CASE. Books

COUNCIL FOR ADVANCEMENT
AND SUPPORT OF EDUCATION®

1307 New York Avenue, NW
Suite 1000
Washington, DC 20005-4701

Table of Contents

Introduction

Why did we write *Advancement Services: Research and Technology Support for Fund Raising?* Simply because there has never been a book written to help those of us working in the operations side of campus fund raising. As Alison Paul mentions in her chapter, nearly every Section 501(c)(3) organization in the United States has a fund-raising program of some form or another, and because of that, we felt there were numerous people who could benefit from this publication.

I recall attending and presenting at my first CASE-sponsored advancement services conference. The year was 1990. The location was Coral Gables, Florida. Thanks to the efforts of Sandra Kidd (then at Emory University) and Ann House (University of Miami), 36 of us gathered to ponder the question: What is advancement services anyway? I am not sure that we have found the answer yet. But based on the 135 or so who annually attend the CASE Summer Institute in Advancement Services, and the 75 or so who attend CASE's Annual Meeting for Chief Advancement Services Professionals, it is clear that more and more of us are trying to figure out who we are!

The nature of our business has changed dramatically during the past decade. Not only have accounting and IRS rules and regulations shaped our direction, but the explosion of newer and faster software and hardware solutions to satisfy our institutional and donor needs have caused us to re-think this business we call advancement services.

For this book, we have called on experts at several universities and state colleges, and others familiar with advancement services issues to obtain advice on the ins and outs of fund raising and how to tackle day-to-day problems that arise within our industry.

You will find, within these chapters, helpful suggestions as well as solutions to everything from dealing with gift processing to working with technology strategies. Prospect tracking and management is now a fundamental component of what we do, so we've included suggestions in this area. We have also touched on IRS rules and regulations along with such concerns as dealing with gifts of securities and matching gifts.

Communication with our donors is essential and it's what keeps our organizations alive and running. We cover topics such as donor relations and how to properly thank our donors for their generosity. However, there are times when we know that a donor is being thanked more than once. This book covers how many thank-you letters is enough and from whom the letter should come.

This book is not about changing your successful methods, but is intended as a tool and a way to give old ideas a fresh approach. I am sure this book will prove to be a useful instrument for your organization and one that you will refer to time and time again. I am proud to have had a role in its creation.

In June, 1991, I wrote an article for CURRENTS entitled "Divine Assistance: A Centralized Financial Services Department Can Be A Heavenly Help to Fund Raisers." Centralized or not, the fact remains that those of us in advancement services make it possible for fund raising to occur. As I concluded in that article, "The ability to complete a financial transaction to development's satisfaction, reduce donor complaints, and guarantee the success of a fund-raising event—these are the true indexes of our performance." I hope this book will help you, and us, perform this function a bit better.

John H. Taylor
June 1999

Advancement Services

Section I

Prospect Research

Chapter 1

Prospect Research: Where It Came From, Where It's Headed

■ By Jonathan Lindsey
Director, Donor Information Services
Baylor University

Art? Science? Combination?
Playing hunches? Taking educated guesses?
All or none of the above?

Research in advancement has come a long way in the past quarter century. Nevertheless, there's still much about it that is hard to define. Even describing a typical workday for a typical researcher is nearly impossible because of the different ways we conduct our work and the different issues that arise from the research enterprise. No two research units are organized or integrated into the advancement process in the same manner.

To grasp the full scope of prospect research, we need to give broad consideration to the significant changes of the past two decades. In this chapter, we'll start with research's conceptual issues, profile, and changing procedures. Following that, we'll turn our attention to the current electronic data deluge. Then we will end this overview of research with a look at the issues the new century will raise, including analysis vs. research, data and data source reliability, trustworthy dipsticks, and the essential quality of our questions.

1. WHERE TWO DECADES OF CHANGE HAVE LED

U ntil the early 1980s, only a few major educational institutions had formal research units in their advancement offices. At about that time, progressive development officers were beginning to recognize the value of market research to direct mail and telemarketing. But particularly in higher education, fund raisers grounded their efforts in class loyalty, reunion class giving programs that grew out of the annual fund, capital campaigns, and other standard activities. Only through careful personal cultivation did development officers explore issues related to giving ability, such as net worth, expendable income, and potential inheritance. The standard literature of the time is replete with warnings not to make assumptions about information the prospect didn't provide.

By combining an entrepreneurial approach with a little academic savvy, enterprising development officers saw an opportunity to focus on an area that had a new feel to it. Research!

In the mid-1980s, however, a not-so-subtle change took place. Thanks to fast-moving cultural issues associated with Wall Street, money became a subject about which even polite persons could converse. Information about money became more public. Concomitantly, but probably unrelated to this cultural phenomenon, advancement offices in large educational institutions began to develop an appreciation for what research could tell about well-known individuals. Development officers who had carefully clipped newspaper articles for their files began to combine that information with knowledge about networking, common board memberships and philanthropic activities, and other facts that provided a critical mass for evaluation.

By combining an entrepreneurial approach with a little academic savvy, enterprising development officers saw an opportunity to focus on an area that had a new feel to it. Research!

Find out what you can about an individual or family. Then look for ways in which their interests coincide with the interests and needs of the campus.

Thus the development/advancement profile was born. One of the first appears in the 1986 CASE book *Prospect Research: A How-to Guide,* edited by Bobby J. Strand and Susan Hunt, which benchmarks the early practices of the field. With the exception of the changes wrought by online data sources, remarkably little has changed. Most institutions still include in their standard prospect profiles such information as name, residential and business addresses and phones, personal history, educational history, special interests, gift history, significant relationships, family history, indications of affinity, philanthropic interests, and other idiosyncratic items deemed necessary at each institution. (For example, one campus had a place on its profile for emotional valence, which a development officer translated as hot buttons.)

Fund-raising staff completed this new instrument after conducting painstaking bibliographic and documentary research in development offices and libraries. A standard check-off list assured that those in training looked for information in all potential resources, duly copied it, and then transcribed it into the profile. Of course, each time the profile was reworked, the whole document had to be retyped. By the mid-1980s, relief came to most advancement offices in the form of word processing. This provided a cut-and-paste environment for creating instantaneous profiles as needed.

Yet another notable step in the development of advancement research was the concomitant advancements in information delivery. Dialog, originally developed for science, began to branch into other areas, such as biographical information. Other databases began to emerge, as did newspaper indexes, so we were no longer dependent on the *New York Times Index* alone. These indexes were at first printed, then microfilmed, and then maintained in digital format.

2. THE ELECTRONIC DATA DELUGE

The microchip spurred the technological advances that in turn prompted significant leaps forward in how we manage information. What was once possible only via massive mainframe computers became easy to do on desktop units that could stand alone or be connected in network configurations. What's more, enterprising computer scientists began to apply business-information data management to the kinds of information advancement services needs, and thus a whole new area of software was born. Here are just a few examples of how technological changes in other realms stimulated further breakthroughs for researchers.

As American industry developed digital modes of inventory control, librarians adapted this type of technology and developed library systems that eventually furthered advancement research.

When business came up with digital methods for maintaining sales records and tracking customer contacts, advancement officers benefited from parallel developments just for them.

At one time, complex data, particularly about securities holdings, was available only in government depositories that required laborious manual research. Once this information was collected in digital formats, it became easily and quickly accessible via mediated online services and then on CD-ROM.

> **A**s we look to the future, one of the significant changes that I hope to see is a shift from being information providers to information analysts.

The combination of easily available financial data, census data (in digital format since 1990), and other information being collected by entrepreneurs has opened another industry: electronic screening. By screening your database electronically, vendors promise to identify wealth indicators that signal near-millionaires, millionaires, and multi-millionaires. Business journals cooperate in this trend by seeking information about significantly rich persons and publicizing that information in lists. Complex formulas now circulate about how to calculate the net worth of an individual or family.

In the mid-1990s, access to information exploded when the Internet became widely popular. While revolutionizing attitudes about how readily available information should be, the Internet created a clear dichotomy between the haves and the have-nots: those with computer access and those without.

All these breakthroughs have led us to have instant access to large quantities of information. Combine that access with an inquisitive mind and a well-trained, computer-literate college graduate, and you have a research revolution. Add to this the sophisticated computer information systems many campuses use to both store and manage information, and you have an advancement revolution.

At the vortex of this revolution is the advancement researcher. This is a person who is normally a college graduate, is computer literate, likes the chase as much as the answer, has an analytical mind, and—oh yes—realizes that the human side of creating the advancement services infrastructure is still immensely important.

3. ISSUES FOR THE NEXT CENTURY

As we look to the future, one of the significant changes that I hope to see is a shift from being information providers to information analysts.

Achieving this change will require intellectual retooling for many of us. We will need to develop skills in interpreting financial data, some of which is extremely complex. We will have to become close followers of business activities, not just those of principal donors or potential donors but of international markets where the ownership is multinational. We may even need to use several languages in the process of filtering and assessing information.

In contrast to the old days, today we no longer have so much trouble finding timely data. Often fresh information is available almost instantly in a variety of electronic sources: home pages, business profiles, industry directories, real estate records, political gifts, auto and luxury item registrations, professional membership directories, and census records. All provide so much data that sifting and analyzing are now vitally important skills. But given the fact that some electronic sources are more reliable than others are, another essential skill is the ability to spot the spurious.

Because of the immense amount of information available on any one individual, some people say conducting research is like looking for a needle in a haystack. But I prefer the metaphor of the automobile dipstick. As we move into the 21st century, we must develop the means to reach directly into the core of information that's relevant to our particular institution. Markers on your dipstick will be similar to the categories that were developed for the advancement research profile during the 1980s. But there will be one significant difference. Synthesizing information, spot-

A Brief History of APRA

To understand how prospect research has emerged as a profession, you need to understand something about the evolution of the Association of Professional Researchers for Advancement (formerly the American Prospect Research Association). APRA provides a distinct professional identity for both hands-on researchers and those who manage that activity as part of advancement services.

The association got its start in the early 1980s when researchers in Minneapolis-St. Paul met to address specific research issues. The first gathering took place June 12, 1981, at Augsburg College in Minneapolis. Members of the group called themselves fund-raising researchers (and briefly considered becoming a sub-unit of the National Society of Fund Raising Executives). By 1983 they took the name Minnesota Prospect Research Association; by 1986 they developed a guiding document about the rights and responsibilities of researchers.

At its July 1987 board meeting, the Minnesota group adopted the name American Prospect Research Association, and on January 11, 1988, APRA was incorporated in Minnesota. The first national meeting took place September 15-16, 1988, at Spring Hill, Minnesota. Looking back at the annual conference topics since then offers a clear indication of the changes that have taken place in technology, in research methodology, and in research's role as the infrastructure for fund raising, particularly in higher education and at medical centers.

Since incorporation, APRA has grown to more than 1,600 members, with approximately half attending meetings in recent years. Leading the organization is a board of directors; it contracts out its membership services and conference management. In 1992, the association adopted a statement of professional ethics that was revised in 1998. In the mid-1990s, the board also considered the question of whether to certify researchers. A task force considered but decided not to pursue certification at that time, and APRA has instead produced basic and advanced skills sets for researchers, tying educational programming to addressing those skills.

Recognizing the fact that research has gone international (as evidenced by members from Canada and Europe), in 1995 the board recommended and the members approved a name change to the Association of Professional Researchers for Advancement.

At the end of its first formal decade, APRA has gained respect for the services these professionals provide and grappled with the impact of a membership sizable enough to need multi-track conferences. The association publishes a professional journal, *Connections,* as well as a newsletter. All these services have earned APRA a distinctive place among the organizations that support the fund-raising profession.

ting relationships, thinking in a matrix, reviewing constituent data, and making suggestions to major gifts officers will require a strong knowledge of advancement protocols in addition to the ability to find information.

The most essential skills we'll bring to our task will be those of the critical questioner. Each research activity will lead to a new set of questions. Knowing wealth indicators is one thing. But we also need to know the history of relationships. Carefully reviewing our own offices' contact reports may lead to valuable information about affinity and ability that external research failed to reveal.

To be a critical questioner will be the challenge in constituent research for the next decade. Achieving the task will require all we can muster in the way of art, science, hunch playing, educated guesses, and highly inquisitive minds.

References

Association of Professional Researchers for Advancement, 414 Plaza Drive, Suite 209, Westmont, IL 60559, (630) 655-0391, apra@adminsys.com.

Strand, Bobby J. and Susan Hunt. *Prospect Research: A How-to Guide.* Washington, DC: CASE, 1986.

Chapter 2

How to Set Up a Research Office: Getting the Go-ahead, Getting Organized, and Getting to Know the Best Sources

■ By Brenda A. Eckles
Director of Development Services
Rhodes College

FIRST THE BASICS: THE FIVE FACETS OF RESEARCH

With any new endeavor, it's always a good idea to remember why you're doing what you're doing. So it is with establishing a research office. Your actions should always be guided by the two underlying purposes of prospect research: to match a prospect's interests and giving ability with your institution's goals and needs, and to preserve over time the institutional memory on a prospect.

Five facets of research contribute to the goal of matching a prospect to an institutional need.

1. Prospect identification. The best place to start is with people or organizations that already have a connection with your institution. For colleges, universities, and independent schools, the most logical groups are trustees, alumni, and parents; other possibilities include local corporations and foundations. Medical charities usually include grateful patients in their prospect identification work. Museums certainly look at their membership rosters. You get the idea. Be creative with your own situation.

2. Prospect screening. Once you've collected the initial prospect pool, individual screening allows you to focus on your best possibilities. The term prospect screening covers several methods for identifying individuals who are both likely to give to your institution and capable of making a major gift. Screening methods include staff or volunteer review, donor group selection, or electronic screening by outside vendors that cross-reference your prospects against information in their databases. Using any or all of these methods should allow you to put your time and resources to best use.

3. Information development. This is the facet that most of us think of first when we think of prospect research. It is the systematic gathering and presentation of useful information in a usable format. Notice I said useful information, not all information. Part of information development is filtering the gathered pieces to include on a profile only those pieces that further the two purposes I mentioned before: matching the prospect to an institutional need and preserving institutional memory.

> *To match a prospect to organizational needs, you must be knowledgeable not only about the prospects but also about your institution.*

4. Prospect classification. The resulting profile should provide the background you need to develop an informed strategy to cultivate and solicit your best prospects. Cultivation steps will vary depending on how involved prospects already are with your institution and what their charitable interests are. The ask amount and purpose will depend on prospects' interests as well as institutional needs. Whether your office should solicit in the near future or many months from now depends on the cultivation process and ask amount. The prospect profile should provide you with the information necessary to properly classify prospects in all these respects.

5. Prospect tracking. The prospect pool must be tracked and managed throughout the cultivation, solicitation, and steward-ship stages. Relevant questions include the following: What culti-vation steps are planned for a prospect and what steps have been completed? Is the time right to ask for a gift? Should a staff mem-ber or a volunteer make the ask?

After the donor makes a gift, stewardship must be managed so that he or she feels good about it. Effective stewardship pre-pares the donor for the next solicitation. A good tracking system maintains and manages all this information.

GETTING STARTED

Two things are certain about setting up a research operation. First, your organization must be willing to commit precious staff and budget to this worthwhile cause. Second, your chief development officer must be convinced of the value of prospect research and be willing and able to make it happen. If your devel-opment leadership is not committed, you might try contacting colleagues at similar institutions and asking them to share suc-cess stories so you can strengthen your case for setting up a research office. Make the case that sound research pays off in more and larger gifts.

Once you have that commitment, what's next? Most research positions include more than just research. My own position has always included information management as well as research; stewardship was added two years ago. Don't let these tasks over-whelm you. Break them down into manageable pieces. As the ancient Chinese philosopher Lao-tzu said, "A journey of a thou-sand miles must begin with a single step."

One of the first steps goes back to the purpose of research. To match a prospect to organizational needs, you must be knowl-edgeable not only about the prospects but also about your insti-tution. You must become as familiar with your institution's mis-sion, goals, and needs as you are with your research tools.

In learning about your institution, it's helpful to find out about the key people who shape it. For me, this meant learning about the governing board, which was the first group I studied when I set up the research shop. I gathered information and developed a prospect profile for each board member. This initial project helped me master prospect research skills and become familiar with a group that plays such an important role in forming institutional goals.

The next group to focus on is major donors who are not on the governing board. The way major donors express their personal interests by making specified gifts will certainly shape the direction of the organization.

There are two things you should begin doing as you gather your institutional knowledge.

1. Start to review two or three local periodicals. Look especially for names of the members of your governing board and major gift donors. This will help you retain those names faster and get you up-to-date on your local community.

2. Set up a research profile form using either a word-processing application or database software. Some development software packages feature a profile module that will fill the need. The profile should include several categories of information. Even though you will almost never gather all of this information for any one prospect, having the categories listed will constantly refresh you as to what information might be helpful to include. For a list of categories, see the box in Table 2-1.

Once you've completed this form during the initial research phase, don't treat it as a closed file. Update it as your office uncovers new information and makes new contacts with the prospective donor.

TARGET YOUR RESEARCH

Focus your efforts by doing prospect screening and by choosing appropriate levels of research for different people. After all, you don't have time to research everyone on your constituency list, and you don't need to research everyone in depth.

The simplest screening method to start off with in a new research office is to target members of specific groups mentioned before: the govern-

---

Table 2-1
What a Prospect Profile Should Cover

Personal Information:
Name, address, phone
Vacation home address and phone and
    periods spent there
Marital status, children, parents, other
    relatives (note any institutional connections)
Date and place of birth
Hobbies/sports/leisure activities

Business Information:
Company, title, address, phone numbers,
    assistants, type of business
Employment history
Corporate board memberships
Professional affiliations

Educational Background:
Class, degree, area of undergraduate,
    graduate, and/or postgraduate study
Honorary degrees

Civic Information:
Civic board memberships
Awards
Social club affiliations

Financial Indicators/Estimates of Wealth:
Salary, stock holdings, property ownership
Inheritances, lifestyle indicators

Philanthropic Information:
Charitable board memberships
Gifts to charities
Volunteer work for charities

Involvement with Your Institution:
Events attended
Volunteer work, including dates
Giving history (detailed)
Liaisons (relatives, friends, business
    colleagues, etc.) and their relationship to
    your institution
Contacts by staff members
Strategy

---

ing board, major donors, and your most effective volunteers. Another good screening idea is to concentrate on staff requests and in-house leads. A new research office is usually awash in staff requests!

As you develop your research operation over time, you may want to consider peer-screening reviews. Peer screening consists of carefully chosen volunteers who review prospective donor names either in a group setting or individually. For people the volunteers know personally, they can advise regarding gift capability as well as interest in your institution.

Another approach to consider as you become established is screening done by outside vendors. Such vendors cross-reference your prospect pool against many kinds of information collected in the vendor database. The firm then presents the results with the goal of identifying the most promising prospects in terms of gift capability. As you might imagine, this can be expensive. Institutions usually do it only in the planning stages of a major campaign.

My office defines three levels of research.

Level I: Basic is simply name, address, phone, business information, and relationship to the institution. We can usually pull this information directly from the computer database.

Level II: Biographical Sketch extends to include family information, educational background, and giving history.

Level III: Complete Profile is a presentation of useful information compiled from all available sources.

WHERE TO LOOK FOR INFORMATION
Traditional Sources

- **Your own office files.** It's hard to know where to look for information when you're first setting up a research operation. Start by determining the sources already available to you. Some of your best information may be waiting in your in-house constituent files. With electronic archives becoming more accessible (many free of charge), paper files of clippings seem to be growing redundant. But don't overlook them. Like me, you may be fortunate to have in-house files of clippings that go back 40 or 50 years or more. Years ago a staff member was thorough in reviewing and clipping local periodicals; I have reaped the benefits of his work time and time again.

In addition to old clippings, staff contact reports can be a rich source of facts. Constantly encourage development officers to write contact reports, and to do so carefully. As in the research profiles, be careful not to step on individuals' privacy rights. Include only facts that are useful to securing a gift or preserving institutional memory, not personal opinions. Remind your colleagues often how valuable contact reports are for continuity despite inevitable staff turnover and changes.

Easily the biggest revolution in prospect research was the development of the Internet.

In-house files often contain other bits of information drawn from surveys or correspondence from the constituent. Surveys sometimes reveal clues to areas of interest for possible gifts as well as attitudes toward your institution. Correspondence can yield several kinds of information, depending on the subject.

- **Volunteers who are close to both your institution and a prospective donor.** In a one-on-one setting, a volunteer who knows and trusts you may feel comfortable talking about the prospective donor and answering some questions. For this reason, you should be included whenever possible in development group meetings that take place with volunteers. By getting to know the best volunteers personally and developing a rapport with them, you'll instill a sense of trust in your professionalism and the value of your work.

If you do take this approach, pick your volunteers carefully. Be certain you select only those who are convinced of the worth of prospect research, and ask only questions that are above reproach. You never want any volunteer to question your motives for gathering information on a prospective donor.

- **Libraries.** A new research office usually has to get established with the barest of budgets. Sometimes it's necessary to stretch your funds by making use of references in nearby municipal or campus libraries.

Periodical indices are invaluable. Other useful general references include the *Who's Who* series of directories, which present biographical sketches on prominent individuals in a region or industry; the local city directory, which gives basic information;

out-of-town city directories; and specialized biographical directories such as *Contemporary Authors*. Most municipal libraries also have a historical section that may include periodical clippings on prominent citizens.

The business section of the library will contain standard references like *Standard & Poor's Register, Dun's Directories, Martindale-Hubbell* (a directory of legal professionals), and the *Directory of Medical Specialists* as well as local business directories.

Public Records

Government public records may disclose property ownership and value. These records are usually housed in county offices. Anyone who visits in person can request information; often county clerks will answer questions by phone, but they aren't required to do so.

Other public documents that prospect researchers sometimes access include probate records. As a will is executed, information outlining the value of the estate and how bequests are distributed to beneficiaries is provided to the court to prove that the executor is carrying out the decedent's instructions. This information becomes public record.

Publicly traded companies are required to make available to the public their Securities and Exchange Commission filings, including annual reports and proxy statements. Proxy statements are a rich source of information regarding compensation and stock ownership of directors and top officers. Most companies will mail these documents at no charge when you phone your request to the investor relations office.

WHERE TO LOOK FOR INFORMATION:
Electronic Sources

Easily the biggest revolution in prospect research was the development of the Internet. Many sources are now available even to researchers with modest budgets. If you work on a campus that already has Internet access, you can obviously connect for free. If not, signing up for Internet access may be the best research money you spend.

- **Free tools.** You have numerous no-cost sources to choose from. For instance, the proxy statements mentioned above are available at no charge via the Internet at the Securities and Exchange Commission World Wide Web site (*www.sec.gov*). Once you've gleaned stock ownership information for directors and top officers from proxy statements, you can get quotes on stock values from several Internet sites, such as Microsoft Investor (*investor.msn.com*).

Every researcher has favorite sites. The Martindale-Hubbell site (*www.martindale.com*) includes free access to its directory of legal professionals, complete with search capabilities. Another of my favorites is the American City Business Journals page (*www.amcity.com*). This site has links to regional business journals across the country as well as a search engine, which allows you to search the entire site or the business journal of a specified city.

- Fee-based sources. Many vendors charge for their information tools. Since new research offices must usually husband their resources carefully, you should thoroughly examine these tools before signing any contracts. With that caveat in mind, here are some sources you may want to investigate.

Of the general-information vendors, Dialog contains probably the largest collection of databases. It covers many of the reference directories cited above as well as a wealth of other information. You can search the databases using a modem connection or through Dialog's Web site (*www.dialog.com*). Each database has variously defined searchable fields and an index database will list databases in which a search phrase yields results. Free training is available to new users in most urban locations; in addition, Dialog has developed user-friendly search capabilities at its Web site.

> *As limited as your time and money may be, you'll still find it worthwhile to invest what you can in conferences, networking opportunities, and periodicals on prospect research.*

Another general-information vendor that's popular with prospect researchers is DataTimes (*www.datatimes.com*), which provides a database of regional newspapers along with similar publications. And while Lexis-Nexis (*www.lexis-nexis.com*) was originally started as a vendor to provide information to legal research offices, it has expanded to users in other disciplines. Like Dialog, it contains reference databases beyond periodical archives.

Some vendors specialize in business and/or financial data. For example, Dow Jones News Retrieval (*www.dj.com*) concentrates in this area. CDA Invest/Net *(www.cda.com/html/cda_invest-net.html)* compiles information gleaned from SEC filings and provides a prospect screening service based on stock holdings of insiders and others. Dun & Bradstreet is one of the best sources on privately held companies. With an Internet presence *(www.dnb.com)* and a desire to expand its customer base, Dun & Bradstreet has begun offering flexible pricing options that make it more attractive to low-volume users. Its most popular report is the *Business Information Report,* which contains a factual summary of information from public records and company officer interviews. Dun & Bradstreet databases are searchable by company name, phone number, or executive name.

A database developed primarily for prospect research is Target America *(www.tgtam.com)*. Information on wealthy Americans is compiled from various sources and used to sort people into wealth categories defined by Target America. Screening can be done in batches or name by name using Internet access. The annual subscription fee is very reasonable, usually within the range of new research shops.

GETTING TRAINING AND PROFESSIONAL DEVELOPMENT

As limited as your time and money may be, you'll still find it worthwhile to invest what you can in conferences, networking opportunities, and periodicals on prospect research. Here are several sources to choose from.

Conferences
- **The Council for Advancement and Support of Education** *(www.case.org)* focuses on fund raisers, alumni administrators, and communications professionals who work at schools, colleges, and independent schools. One of its best offerings for prospect researchers is its Annual Conference for Development Researchers, a two- to three-day program. Another popular conference, the week-long Summer Institute in Advancement Services, covers prospect research as well as other service functions, such as gift processing and stewardship. And in 1998, CASE began offering an online program, Prospect Research on the Internet.

Organized around a core curriculum framework, the electronic courses typically offer how-to training over five weeks.

You can also get individual sessions on research as well as broader networking opportunities at CASE's eight district conferences, which take place regionally from December to April, and its Annual Assembly, offered each July.

- **The Association for Professional Researchers in Advancement** *(weber.u.washington.edu/~dlamb/apra/APRA.html)* hosts an international conference each summer devoted to prospect research topics. Workshops include beginner, advanced, technology, and management tracks. In addition, vendor exhibits, a computer lab (you can try fee-based vendors free!), and a model library give you hands-on experience with a variety of research resources. The association also offers regional conferences sponsored by more than 25 chapters nationwide. These feature inexpensive local programs in one- and two-day sessions.

Also note APRA's mentor program, which links veteran researchers with ones who have limited experience or are new to a region or type of nonprofit. These partnerships are designed to provide one-on-one support as researchers set up and manage their operations.

- **The National Society of Fund Raising Executives** *(www.nsfre.org)* serves development officers at a broad range of nonprofits. NSFRE runs prospect research tracks at its national conference and usually at local chapter workshops as well.

- **Development consulting firms** often sponsor workshops or one-on-one training sessions. If your institution has a contractual relationship with a firm, you may be able to participate.

Listservs

These days, some of the best networking takes place on free electronic mail discussion lists. Prospect researchers have their own group, Prospect-L (pronounced prospect-ell). To subscribe, send an e-mail to *listserv@bucknell.edu*. In the message, *type subscribe prospect-l* and your real name. To post a message to the subscriber group, send an e-mail to *prspct-l@bucknell.edu*.

As you might expect, subscribers on the various discussion lists range from novices to seasoned professionals. Some lists generate many messages, usually more than you'll be able to read and still get your job done! Protect your limited time by using the subject line to cull messages; read only those in which you have an interest or need. (To see a list of other e-mail discussion groups in which you might be interested, visit *weber.u.washington.edu/ ~dlamb/apra/lists.htm.*).

> *These days, some of the best networking takes place on free electronic mail discussion lists.*

Periodicals

Some of the professional associations mentioned above offer publications as a benefit of membership. CURRENTS, a monthly magazine published by CASE, covers topics in prospect research several times each year. APRA publishes *Connections*, a quarterly journal devoted exclusively to prospect research. You don't need to join an association to subscribe to the *Chronicle of Philanthropy*, an every-other-week trade newspaper that often publishes articles on research trends.

A LAST WORD ABOUT INTEGRITY

The old Aretha Franklin song says it all: R-E-S-P-E-C-T for the prospect should always be foremost in your mind. Confidentiality is a must in all development work, and certainly in prospect research.

To help you set standards, it's smart to write a research policy for your office, and to do it sooner rather than later. Researchers at peer institutions are usually willing to share such documents. Your chief development officer and office colleagues will probably want to provide input. The CASE Advisory on Advancement Practice: Principles and Recommendations, which covers ethics and confidentiality, may be useful as you write your policy. Once you've got it, review it annually for needed revisions.

But no matter what, make certain all your files are secure, both on computer and on paper. Share research profiles only on a need-to-know basis, and only with development staff. If a volunteer needs some of the information, write a meeting brief containing only the facts the volunteer must have to do the task requested. Even then, guard confidentiality closely.

Finally, when writing a research profile, include no unnecessary information. Here we end with the principles with which we began. You must be familiar with all aspects of development to make good judgments about what is valuable information and what you should not include in a research profile. In all your work, remember the purpose of prospect research: to match a prospect's interests and giving capability with your institution's goals and needs, and to preserve over time the institutional memory on a prospect.

References

Bergen, Helen. *Where the Information Is: A Guide to Electronic Research for Nonprofit* Organizations. Alexandria, VA: BioGuide Press, 1996. 257 pages.

Hall, Holly. "Many Charities Collect Useless Data on Potential Donors, Researchers Are Told," *Chronicle of Philanthropy,* Vol. 5, No. 22 (September 7, 1993): 38.

Hudson, Michel. Prospect Research Fundamentals. Sioux City, IA: Stevenson Consultants Inc., 1997. 46 pages.

McNamee, Mike. "Privacy and the Prospect Researcher," CURRENTS, Vol. 16, No. 6 (June 1990): 10-

Ryan, Ellen. "Making the Most of the World Wide Web: How the Internet is Helping Prospect Researchers Find New Information and Share It with Colleagues," CURRENTS, Vol. 22, No. 6 (June 1996): 50-

Strand, Bobbie J. "Getting a Payback from Online Services: How You Can Make the Most of Your Time and Money When Using Fee-Based Prospect Research Services," CURRENTS, Vol. 22, No. 6 (June 1996): 52-

Strand, Bobbie J. and Hunt, Susan. *Prospect Research: A How-to Guide.* Edited by Bobbie J. Strand and Susan Hunt. Washington, DC: CASE, 1986. 150 pages.

Chapter 3

Organizing and Using Research: From Setting Up Prospect Profiles to Calculating Giving Ability

■ By Claire Verrette
Manager, Major Gifts
Texas Medical Association Foundation
(Former Director of Prospect Research
George Washington University)

Congratulations! You have a nice large stack of paper full of information about a good prospect. But what do you do with it? How do you organize it in a meaningful way? Once you have it organized, then what do you do?

Sometimes answering these questions is even harder than doing the research itself. You might have so much information that you find it difficult to organize and present. On the other hand, you may have so little that you don't feel you can make a judgment regarding the prospect's viability (much less estimate an ask amount).

But as an advancement services professional, it is your

responsibility to facilitate development by presenting research in a clear, consistent manner. Your fund raisers should not have to comb through irrelevant or disorganized facts to determine exactly who a prospect is and why they should care. Nor should they have to blindly stab at an ask amount. You can help with an initial estimate, even if you have very little financial information.

To help you out, in this chapter we will discuss two issues: how to organize your information in a useful and meaningful manner and, once that's done, how to interpret and evaluate your data. From categorizing your findings to figuring net worth, all of these techniques should help you prepare your fund-raising colleagues for successful solicitations.

GETTING RESEARCH READY TO USE

There are two keys to organizing research. First, make it as user-friendly as possible. Know your users and their preferences. Research is, after all, a service, which means always keeping the customer in mind. Second, know your technology. Whatever your format, you don't want to spend more time inputting and extracting data than you spend on the research process.

When designing forms, ask the following questions. When your development officers request information about a prospect, what is the first question they ask? What is the last? Do they prefer narrative form or bullets? Do you have the ability to store most of the information in your computer database? Even more important, do you have the ability to get it out?

Finally, are you always going to do full profiles, including anything and everything, or are there times when briefer is better? You may want to create different versions. When I worked at George Washington University, we had four:

- **Memoranda,** to answer one or two specific questions.
- **Level I,** which includes verified name, address, spouse, occupation, relationship to GW, and GW giving history.
- **Level II,** which includes all of the previous information plus a biographical picture, GW contact summary, assessed value of primary residence, and business and community affiliations.

• **Level III,** which covers the previous information plus complete biographical and financial pictures, including land and property ownership, legal data, and stock holdings reported to the Securities and Exchange Commission.

There are as many ways to format a profile as there are development officers and researchers—and probably more. (For example, you'll find a variation on my list in Chapter 2, Table 2-1.) It's probably impossible to design a profile that everybody loves. However, most researchers include standard categories like the ones I've listed in Table 3-1.

When developing research profiles, start by listing the categories you use. Then add any others you find appropriate and helpful. For instance, have you done an electronic screening of your database? Include this data.

Next, determine your format. Put your list of categories in order according to your fund raisers' needs. It's that simple. You may want to create a template from your word-processing program, or you may prefer to create the form on a database program. I know one organization that has everything in Lotus Notes so the staff can include or omit categories as needed. Many organizations create records using programs such as Microsoft Access. Ideally, you should be able to enter all data into your development database. Just remember that you need to be able to get the data out, too! If you can't, then don't use the information.

A final note regarding organizing your research: This may seem obvious, but when you actually input the information, start at the beginning. Thinking in a logical manner helps you organize those piles and piles of research.

EVALUATING WHAT YOU'VE GATHERED

Evaluating research is both a science and an art. Even though many "scientific" formu-

---

Table 3-1
Standard Profile Information

Name

Birthplace and date

Family information: spouse and children

Education

Profession/occupation, including career history and company information

Financial information (salary, real estate, securities, and other assets)

Corporate affiliations

Foundation affiliations

Other affiliations: nonprofits, memberships, professional, etc.

Awards and special honors

Relationship to institution, including
    Major and degree (if an education institution)
    Alumni activities (ditto)
    Student activities (ditto)
    Volunteer activities (e.g., working with career development or admissions)
    Giving history
    Internal ratings and external ratings
    Contacts with development and other staff
        Known relationships with other alumni

Known giving to other organizations and political campaigns

Other/miscellaneous

---

las are available, ultimately a fair amount of artistry will be involved. This is because you can't be completely sure of either of the two most important factors: money or the people who possess it. Not only is financial information usually limited and incomplete, but people tend to be unpredictable. You can never know for sure if prospects will make a commitment until they actually do so.

However, it is advisable to devise some system, formal or informal, for evaluating your research. It doesn't work to throw together a list of a thousand names and tell the fund raisers to call every single one. Instead, help identify and rank the good prospects and weed out the less than ideal ones.

Research can be an important element of strategic planning when you use it to answer questions regarding relationships, approach, and ask amount. You can get insights into all three by taking what's called the CIA approach to ranking prospects.

CIA: Contact, Interest, and Ability

Ultimately, you want to rank your prospects from top to bottom—that is, beginning with your best prospects (those most likely to make the largest gifts) and descending to your long-shot prospects (those with the least ability and likelihood). The guidelines in Table 3-2 are adapted from an article by Kim Klein in the *Grassroots Fundraising Journal* (and reproduced on the World Wide Web site, *www.allianceonline.org/*.)

Contacts and Interest

It's especially important to have a good understanding of prospects' relationship to your institution. If your prospects have no interest in giving to you, it won't matter if they're as rich as Rockefeller. Likewise, if they might be interested but you cannot get through to them, then you are less likely to get the gift. So review your research to get an idea of the breadth and depth of the prospect's involvement with your institution.

First, examine contacts. That is, whom does your prospect know (or who knows your prospect), and in what capacity? Are the contacts with advancement

---

Table 3-2

How to Prioritize Your Prospects

Category A: Previous givers who are prospects for a repeat or upgraded gift
1. Donors with strong relationships—as volunteers, in leadership, etc.
2. Regular givers who otherwise are not active.
3. Recent but sporadic givers.

Category B: Nongivers who are close to someone in the organization
1. Those with an interest in the cause (i.e., they haven't given to Alpha University but do have an interest in education).
2. Those who haven't demonstrated interest either through giving or activity.

Category C: People who are interested in the cause but don't know anyone in the organization

Source: Kim Klein, Grassroots Fundraising Journal, Vol. 2, No. 5

staff, faculty or other staff, board members, students (in the case of parents), or others (e.g., doctors at a hospital)? How close are these contacts? In other words, whose phone calls would be returned, and who would best relate to the prospect?

Next, evaluate the level of interest in the institution and in the cause. Begin by reviewing the following:

- **Prior giving—patterns and source (direct mail, personal solicitation, special events).**
  1. Best prospects have given fairly regularly and increased their gift size; ones who've given more without being solicited deserve special note.
  2. The next best have given regularly with no increase in gift size.
  3. The rest have given sporadically and/or at a significant level.
- **Activities.** The general rule is to rank by level of activity (e.g., board membership) and frequency of interaction (as well as how recently). For instance, at the top of your list are those with current board, committee, and other leadership positions. Next are those who regularly attend and/or volunteer for special events or are involved in other volunteer activities (e.g., working with admissions or career development).
- **External factors** are a bit more difficult because this information can be sporadic. You will not always uncover news of a family foundation or long articles about your prospects' philanthropic interests. However, you should make an effort to look for any clues, such as board affiliations, known giving to other organizations, etc.

Ability: Art, Craft, or Science?

The standard factors in determining potential gift size are prior giving, net worth and/or known assets, interest level, and donations to other organizations. There is a plethora of formulas available for the first two, so we'll explore those in some depth below. You can factor in the latter two as appropriate.

A note regarding the formulas that follow: Different ones bring different results, which can vary widely. You may have to experiment before you decide which to follow.

1. Prior Giving Formulas

To determine a solicitation amount, start with this. Here are two of the most commonly used formulas (for major gifts or campaign gifts given over five years):

- Strong interest and likelihood: 20 times prior consistent annual giving. In other words, quadruple the gift size multiplied for five years. For example, if a prospect has been making annual gifts of $500, the ask amount would be $500 X 4 X 5 years = $10,000.
- Relatively strong interest and likelihood: 10 times prior consistent annual giving. For example, $500 X 2 X 5 = $5,000.

2. Net Worth and Known Asset Formulas

If you surveyed 100 random groups of researchers, you would probably find a 50-50 split. One group would firmly believe in the viability of net worth estimates. The other would believe the best you can do is to uncover indicators of wealth and leave it at that.

The remaining 20 percent work somewhere in between the two camps. These researchers use financial data as an important piece in prospect qualification. They might provide an initial estimate for giving ability but leave the final estimate to the development officer.

Regardless of which camp you fall into (or have signed up for), you do need to know what the fuss is about.

What do we mean when we talk about net worth? The definition is simple: assets minus liabilities. However, it's impossible to get a full picture of both. An additional complication is that formulas based on this information make assumptions about market stability, distribution of assets, life stage, and prospect interest—assumptions that may or may not be valid.

The U.S. Department of Commerce Bureau of the Census regularly studies the asset ownership of households. They estimate the elements of net worth and

Table 3-3

Asset Distribution for the Typical Household

Asset	Proportion of Net Worth
Home ownership	44%
Interest-earning assets at financial institutions	11%
Stocks and mutual fund shares	8%
Rental property	7%
IRA or KEOGH accounts	7%
Motor vehicles	6%
Business or profession	6%
Other real estate	5%
Other interest earning assets	4%
Other financial investments	3%
U.S. savings bonds	1%
Checking accounts	1%

Source: U.S. Department of Commerce Bureau of the Census

their distribution as you see them in Table 3-3.

These census figures are from 1993, but a review of prior years shows that they vary little from survey to survey. The primary change has been the proportionate increase in the worth of home equity, stocks and mutual fund shares, and U.S. savings bonds. (Note: Because unsecured liabilities are subtracted from the distribution of net worth, the percentages add up to more than 100 percent.)

As you can see, very few of these ingredients can be easily researched and absolutely known. In the case of both assets and liabilities, much of this is private information. Usually you can uncover some information regarding real estate, and you can learn stock information if the prospect is an insider trader (defined as holding 5 percent or more of a company's stock or holding the position of officer or director). At times, salary information is available or can be reasonably estimated. But learning about other assets is hit or miss (and generally the latter).

Even so, there are other sources that can help you make an educated guess. The Internal Revenue Service regularly studies personal wealth as well. One such study focuses on the distribution of assets for what the IRS calls top wealth holders—those adults with gross assets of at least $600,000. These 4.1 million individuals account for 2 percent of the total U.S. population. The IRS data is extrapolated from estate tax returns. For instance, a recent IRS analysis demonstrates a number of differences in asset distribution among the wealthy, primarily in overall diversification and a more even distribution of assets.

In addition, the study details the difference in distribution by gender and age. For instance, the figures demonstrate that men have a higher percentage of their assets in stocks than women do. For men, the average is 29.5 percent of total assets in stocks, and over half of those in closely held stocks. Real estate is generally 24.6 percent, and cash makes up 5.3 percent of assets.

Women tend to have a closer distribution: 26.7 percent in stocks and 26.7 percent in real estate. In addition, female investors keep a higher percentage of stock investments in bonds and mutual funds, and a higher percentage of their real estate investments are in personal residences. However, for women, cash is 7.1 percent of assets.

Researchers have long used the data from this series of studies to determine their formulas for estimating net worth or giving ability. Few use formulas that specify gender, but a couple of them use age.

Indeed, when evaluating any financial data, it is important to consider the prospect's stage in life. The following questions are loosely based on a presentation by Karen Osborne of The Osborne Group, Inc. To determine an individual's standing, ask yourself:

- Is your prospect just starting out—someone who owns fewer assets, none very liquid, and makes gifts out of discretionary income? This will most likely be an *annual donor.*
- Is she or he acquiring lifestyle—buying a second home, sending children to preparatory school, taking luxury vacations—someone with more assets, high income, but an expensive lifestyle? This may mean larger gifts, perhaps, but the prospect is probably still using discretionary income to make gifts.
- Is the prospect well-established—someone who has reached a point in his or her life when it's time to consider disbursing income and liquid assets? Sometimes this is tied to age, but not always.
- The final stage is when a prospective donor is considering disbursing assets and making estate plans. This is the stage when an ultimate gift is often considered.

Crunching the net worth numbers
Formulas for net worth estimates tend to use the data most available to researchers: income, stock holdings, and real estate. The following are some of the most popular formulas, by data type.

Income
Net worth = (age X total income) divided by 10.

Total income is defined as salary, dividends, payments for board meetings, etc. This is the formula used by authors Stanley and Danko in *The Millionaire Next Door.* Rick Snyder of the University of Vermont put together a spreadsheet that calculates this; you can access it in the financial research section on the UVM website *(www.uvm.edu/~gcargill/research/ research.html).* Also on this page, you can link to a spreadsheet that directly calculates the rating by age and income. Synder recommends that those of us who are less affluent may not want to try this using our salaries—it won't work.)

Stock holdings
Net worth = direct stock holdings X 1, 2, or 3

This formula was suggested by Angela Vaughan of the University of Virginia in the winter 1998 issue of *The Prospector,* the newsletter of the Virginia chapter of the Association for Prospect Researchers in Advancement. (It was later republished on the UVa research department's Web site: *www.people. virginia.edu/~dev-pros/Networth.html).* Fans of this formula have found it to be reliable. If it looks like a majority of the prospect's assets are in stock holdings, then they use a lower multiplier. If the prospect seems to have more diversified asset distribution, they use a higher one.

If I have a prospect who is clearly affluent and well established, I might use a multiplier of 3, 4, or 5, assuming that stock is likely to be anywhere from 20 to 33 percent of worth, depending on age, gender, and profession. As recommended by Rob Millar in the July/August 1995 CURRENTS article called "How Much Is That Donor in Your Records," I have used the IRS statistics in this determination. Thus, for example, if we assume that individuals' stocks are 25 percent of their portfolio, then the multiplier would be 4. This is based on the IRS's estimated distribution of assets for top wealth holders.

Real estate
Net worth = total holdings X 3, 4, or 5

Again, I turned to the University of Virginia. Vaughan recommended a multiplier of 5 for real estate worth $400,000 and above. Thus, real estate worth $400,000 X 5 would meet the minimum. Real estate holdings worth less than $400,000 are multiplied by 3. UVa's research had determined that this was more accurate at that level. This also fits when using the IRS statistics.

Estimating Gift Potential Over Five Years			
Net Worth	**At 1%**	**At 2.5%**	**At 5%**
$100,000	$1,000	$2,500	$5,000
$200,000	$2,000	$5,000	$10,000
$500,000	$5,000	$12,500	$25,000
$750,000	$7,500	$18,750	$37,500
$1 million	$10,000	$25,000	$50,000
$5 million	$50,000	$125,000	$250,000
$10 million	$100,000	$250,000	$500,000
$25 million	$250,000	$625,000	$1.25 million
$50 million	$500,000	$1.25 million	$2.5 million
$100 million	$1 million	$2.5 million	$5 million
$500 million	$5 million	$12.5 million	$25 million

Figure 3-1
Estimating Giving Ability with Standard Percentages

3. GIVING ABILITY FORMULAS

Once you've figured the net worth estimate, you can estimate giving ability. There are several ways to do this.

A. Estimating gift potential using standard percentages

Many fund raisers traditionally assume a major gift ability of 5 percent of net worth. I prefer to use a range of 1 to 5 percent to account for interest levels. For GW, I devised the chart in Figure 3-1. But even it is somewhat arbitrary. You may find that different percentages work for you.

B. Estimating gift potential using known assets

Working directly with assets makes for quicker qualification when prospecting. I've used the following formulas to determine the minimum amounts of assets a prospect must have to be considered a campaign prospect. These minimums have helped us when using the data we received from an electronic screening. For example, if I'm looking for prospects capable of a minimum of $50,000 over five years, I might use the following criteria:

- **Income:** minimum $500,000 (this could include salary, bonus, director's fees, etc.). Note: I informally account for regional variations. For instance, for a New Yorker, I'd look for a higher salary.
- **Stock holdings:** minimum $1 million, preferably $2 million to $5 million.
- **Real estate:** minimum $250,000. Again, I account for regional differences.
- **Private company sales:** minimum $4 million.

Or a combination of the above.

To arrive at these formulas, I used the formulas detailed below. Since these formulas use definitely known information, I feel more secure in my estimate. Also, I can do my math in one step to save time, multiplying the known financial information by one of the following to estimate gift size (as opposed to figuring net worth, then using an additional multiplier).

C. Gift potential formulas by data type

Income

I use 10 percent and continue to do so if we have a good relationship with the donor. Rob Millar cited this figure in his CURRENTS article. He based it on previous *Giving USA* reports that Americans gave away an average of nearly 2 percent of their income. However, the most recent *Giving USA* reported that the average was down to 1.6 percent, so you might want to change your routine figures to 8 percent, saving 10 percent for prospects who have strong interest.

Rick Snyder's spreadsheet is especially useful for this because he breaks it out by age and income, thus accounting for some age difference. However, when you're looking at younger prospects, they're probably in the asset-building stage of life and still making most of their gifts with discretionary income. Therefore, they would be likely to give a lower percentage of their income to charity. Likewise, someone who is more established could give away more income.

Stock holdings (and other relatively liquid assets)

There are several options for these. The lowest percentage I have seen is 0.05 percent, and the highest is 15 percent. The following are some possibilities.

- Rob Millar recommends assuming different percentages for different levels of holdings. This is definitely worth considering because holdings of $500,000 to $1 million (or even a bit more) are very likely to be a part of your prospect's retirement kitty. Thus they aren't as likely to give such a high percentage because they wouldn't want to give away a future income source. On the other hand, if the prospect is facing a capital gains tax, it can be advantageous to make such a gift. Once again, using judgment is important.

    1% to 4% for holdings worth $1 to $499,999
    5% to 9% for holdings worth $500,000 to $999,999
    10% for holdings worth $1 million

- Another option is to work the figures such as the ones from the University of Virginia to a direct number; Virginia's numbers work out to 5 to 15 percent. Some institutions consider that high and recommend 0.5 to 1.5 percent. When deciding on a formula, you need to look at your donors' giving patterns and decide which works best for you. For my part, making the initial qualification while prospecting, I prefer a conservative figure of 5 percent, especially given potential stock market volatility.

Real estate
I usually use a figure between 5 and 20 percent. If you translate the Virginia figures, you get 9 percent of total real estate holdings for below $400,000 and 25 percent for above $600,000.

Private company ownership
This is one of the most difficult figures to assess. The challenge is to determine the value of the company and the prospect's equity in it. Researchers usually devise a minimum based on their own experience and a formula such as the one below. It's advisable to be a bit conservative in your calculations because private company ownership isn't necessarily as liquid.

Once again, we turn to a formula from Rob Millar that is based on a formula from *Fortune* magazine. If you assume that an individual's equity in a company is at least 25 to 50 percent of the value of that company, you can then figure a gift of 1.5 to 5 percent of that equity. The question is: What is the value of the company? Although Dun & Bradstreet reports offer a figure, it does not necessarily reflect sale price. Unless you know otherwise, stick to a value equal to sales. Thus, a prospect who has equity in a company with $4 million in sales might have a net worth in the company of $1 million to $2 million. Therefore, that individual could make a gift of at least $50,000.

Combination
At times you'll have several of the above pieces. In that case, you could figure each net worth estimate based on the assets, then use the average to figure overall net worth or gift capacity. Alternatively, you might prefer to figure each giving-ability estimate based on the assets and then use the average for net worth.

Karen Osborne of the Osborne Group has suggested the guidelines to use when soliciting major gifts in Figure 3-2, which combines income and assets. It doesn't follow the above formulas exactly, but it does give you an idea of a useful approach.

Osborne recommends that you consider a number of additional factors in determining the appropriate "ask" amount. These may include, but not be limited to: the donor's ability to replace assets, past history of giving (to your institution as well as other institutions), the prospect's time window (factors that include age, availability of disposable income, family obligations, etc.), source of the prospect's wealth, and so on.

Gift Over Time	Minimum Income	Minimum Assets
$10,000	$50,000	$200,000
$25,000	$100,000	$500,000
$50,000	$250,000	$500,000
$100,000	$250,000	$1,000,000
$500,000	$500,000	$5,000,000
$1,000,000	$500,000	$10,000,000

Figure 3-2
Using Income and Assets to Figure Giving Ability

Source: Karen E. Osborne, The Osborne Group, Inc.

There are a number of additional formulas you could apply to this process. No matter which ones you choose, evaluating your research should always go further than number crunching. Remember, we are dealing with people, so it's important to look for Contacts, Interest, *and* Ability. Ability alone will not bring in the gifts.

Four final tips on calculating giving ability

1. Create your own prospect criteria and/or tables, based on your own organization's constituencies.

2. Factor in the current state of the real estate and stock markets. Also check particular stocks' current health.

3. Always temper ability with previous giving. It doesn't matter if your prospect is capable of $1 million gifts if he or she consistently declines to upgrade from $100 annual gifts.

4. Factor in prior relationship and potential relationship. In other words, you might legitimately be more optimistic if you know the prospect has a strong affinity and less optimistic if there has been no prior relationship.

TAKING THE NEXT STEP

You've researched your top prospects and know they meet your minimum criteria. Next you need to put it all together. You need to rank your prospects according to ability, likelihood, and readiness.

There are different schools of thought regarding how much you as the researcher should be involved in ratings, but you can at least establish initial ability ratings and work with the development officers regarding likelihood and readiness. In any case, this is the time to assign the best prospects to development officers and create initial strategies. Now is the time for moves (or portfolio) management.

References

Johnson, Barry W. "Personal Wealth, 1992-1995," *Statistics of Income Bulletin,* Internal Revenue Service, 1997/1998 Winter: pp. 70-83.

Klein, Kim. "The Fine Art of Asking for the Gift," *Grassroots Fundraising Journal,* Vol. 2, No. 5. Reproduced by the Clearinghouse for Nonprofit Management on its Web site, *www.igc.org/sca.*

Millar, Robert G., III "How Much Is That Donor in Your Records?" CURRENTS, July/August 1995: pp. 38-42.

Osborne, Karen E., Principal, The Osborne Group, Inc., 70 West Red Oak Lane, White Plains, New York, NY 10604. (914) 697-4921.

Vaughan, Angela. "Estimating Net Worth: One Organization's Search for Truth," *The Prospector,* Winter 1998. Reproduced for the APRA-Virginia Web site, *www.people.Virginia.edu/~dev-pros/NETWORTH.html.*

Stanley, Thomas J. and William D. Danko. *The Millionaire Next Door: The Surprising Secrets of America's Wealthy.* Longstreet Press; October, 1996. 258 pages.

"What We're Worth," *Bureau of the Census Statistical Brief,* U.S. Department of Commerce, November 1995.

Chapter 4

The Moves-Management System: An Overview for Advancement Services Professionals

■ By Judson Matthews
Alumni Development Consultant
Systems and Computer Technology Corporation
(formerly Director of Advancement Services, The Citadel)

What is a moves-management system? It's a tool that can help to identify, establish, cultivate, solicit, and steward relationships between an organization and its prospective donors. A prospect "moves" through a series of planned and coordinated activities with the expectation of a positive outcome: a gift.

Moves management is resource-intensive because it requires time, staff, and dollars. Therefore, most fund-raising offices use it primarily for major gift prospects. In this chapter, we'll concentrate on using moves management for these prospects, with a special emphasis on promoting teamwork among all the individuals in your organization. As an advancement services professional, you'll probably be most involved in identification and stewarding. But because you'll also be part of the team, you need to understand the following five moves-management components: planning, the prospect pool, support and staffing, an information tracking system, and defined policies and procedures.

1. PLANNING

Planning donor moves requires building a consensus about which prospects to follow and the need to share reliable information about them. When I worked at The Citadel, my office encouraged this by staying in constant communication with the offices of the president and academic dean as well as public relations, athletics, and alumni affairs. These departments provided us with invaluable information about trips, contacts, or events (on-campus and off-campus) for various college officials. Our office made a point of calling on other offices to gather helpful information, which let us champion our goals to others who have an impact, directly or indirectly, on our ability to succeed.

You don't want to get bogged down in the planning process, but you do need to think through your moves-management system from A to Z, in this case from prospect to satisfied donor. And you need to put your thoughts in writing!

Again, if I had to choose just one word to describe the key to success, it would be teamwork. Start by assessing who will use the system. Possibilities include development officers, the administration (your president or VP), your organization's computer support, system analysts, and other members of your office. Once you've identified all the areas that will be involved, no matter how small, choose a representative from each. The representative should be someone who's a team player; who asks "why" and "what can we do to improve the system"; and who has strong interpersonal skills, an understanding of their area, and an understanding of the objective of the system.

As you begin to identify prospects and plan your donor moves, ask representatives of each area to express their expectations of their roles and of the system. The planning phase allows all the system's users and supporters to gain an understanding of each other's role.

2. THE PROSPECT POOL

To build a prospect pool, gather information from the following areas:

1. Your development office (research staff, development officers, annual fund staff, gift processing and records).

2. Other staff (president, department heads, alumni office, etc.).

3. Volunteers and boards (the board of visitors, advisory boards, class chairs, reunion committees, alumni clubs, etc.).

4. Supporting organizations (foundations, if applicable).

5. Outside references (library, online services, World Wide Web, government records—including local, state, and federal—newspapers and magazines, etc.).

With continuous input from the above areas and any others that are relevant to your situation, you should be able to compile a profile for each prospect. In addition to showing a donor's personal and professional relationships, profiles will give you a great starting point to identify the interests your donor and your organization have in common. For examples of how these profiles can work, see Chapters 2 and 3. The profile will be essential for helping you plan the next move, whether it's identification, cultivation, or solicitation.

3. SUPPORT AND STAFFING
Getting buy-in from your administration

It's been proven time and again that your most effective fund raisers are your top administrators—your president or executive director, deans, or vice presidents. A moves-management system will let you use their skills and talents to best advantage.

The appropriate individual from your office should meet in person with each of the key individuals within your administration to discuss the importance of their support for fund raising. Make sure you cover:

- the benefits of fund raising, such as financing a new piece of equipment, program, or building;
- the process of fund raising (relationship building) through interest, involvement, and investing;

- the level of commitment needed in terms of time, appearances, and availability; and
- the importance of improved communication throughout the organization.

At The Citadel, all of our advancement directors once took part in a great team-building activity: a retreat with our board of visitors to share what we do and what we need from them. Their response was overwhelming. The board and staff walked away having established a personal rapport.

Once you've laid the groundwork with senior staff and volunteers, moves management will:
- allow you to match up prospective donor interests with appropriate members of your administration and staff;
- provide your administration with a time-management tool for fund raising; and
- improve communication and keep your administration informed.

Staffing your system

Depending upon whom you ask, ratios of major gift prospects to fund raisers will vary. Some say you should have 200 prospects to each fund raiser; others will say the ratio should be 50:1 or even fewer. Your office must assess for itself the optimal number of prospects that your development officers can effectively—and I emphasize *effectively*—handle.

To see my point, consider this typical routine to get one $50,000 gift. Successfully soliciting one gift requires three to five prospects. Typically, you need to conduct six to nine moves per prospect. Therefore, you will need to manage 18 to 45 moves just for one $50,000 gift. What if you were in a capital campaign?

It's quite possible to have several development officers communicating with a prospect. A moves-management system serves as a communication tool for them. However, most organizations assign a specific prospect manager to each donor. Your prospect manager(s) should be the gatekeeper for all moves on their prospects—period! The manager's role is threefold: to ensure communication and coordination between members of your staff and organization, to ensure the prospect is being moved through the system, and to evaluate the effectiveness of the moves on the prospect's relationship.

The manager is also responsible for coordinating volunteers. Volunteers are instrumental in gathering research, coordinating special events, cultivating a prospect, and serving as part of the solicitation team. You should establish a plan for using and managing volunteers with defined responsibilities, timeline, and measurable goals.

4. AN INFORMATION TRACKING SYSTEM

M ost software designed specifically for fund raising has built-in tracking systems for prospect management. Even so, the tracking system serves only as a tool; you must tailor it to fit your organization's needs and available resources. There is no one-size-fits-all system. To read more about choosing the right system for prospect management, see Chapters 12, 13, and 14.

Training

This is one of the most critical components of moves management. Without proper training, your system will not be fully utilized and may actually become a hindrance. If it's difficult and time-consuming to use, you may find that your development officers become frustrated and even set up their own prospect-management systems.

To avoid this, the training mandate should come from the top down. Upper management should support, require, and also attend training to demonstrate its importance. Even so, higher-ups should take care to avoid issuing orders along the lines of "you *will* use this system." It's more productive to create an environment for sharing ideas. Everyone from users to management should view training as an opportunity to understand the hows and whys of the system—and to treat learning as an ongoing process.

Disseminating information

Your system's effectiveness depends on how easily everyone can access information, whether electronic or written.

Finding Out Who Needs What

W hen I do training, here are the questions I ask trainees beforehand.
- What type of information do you need?
- How do you plan to use this information?
- How would you like for the information to be distributed (viewed)?
- What are your frustrations with the current system?

Once I have this information, I design a customized plan that addresses the concerns and/or topics the trainees have identified. I also tailor the training to make it as convenient as possible for them, especially when it comes to time and place.

I recommend storing, retrieving, and sharing all information electronically. Not only can such information as donor profiles, contact reports, and organizational literature be stored and retrieved quickly, but more important, accuracy and security are improved and complete donor files are available in a few seconds.

There are numerous PC-based and mini- and mainframe-based software packages available. We work closely with our information technology department to ensure that our systems are consistent with its objectives and compatible with its campus-wide systems (such as e-mail, Internet access, etc.).

5. DEFINED POLICIES AND PROCEDURES

These provide a consistent framework in which to operate the system. Policies and procedures should address the following areas:

Standard terms and routines

- **The definition of a move:** This may seem basic, but it's necessary. If you don't define what constitutes an initiative or contact, you may find yourself with useless information within your system—and disorganized information outside it. I define a move as an exchange of information between prospect and organizational representative, as a result of which your organization has the opportunity to initiate a new action with the prospect.
- **How to share information:** Define a chain of command to process (coordinate, review, and distribute) incoming and outgoing communication/information (reports, correspondence, and conversations). Be sure to include the president's office, the offices of your deans or VPs, your department heads, board members, staff, and donors. Some of the most difficult decisions we've had to make about sharing or passing on information have involved the politics associated with donors or our administration. By defining and approving communication protocol, you minimize potential backlash and have a consistent policy.
- **Users and their responsibilities.** Ensure that you have each action or task, no matter how small, clearly defined and written down. Otherwise you run the risk of confusion and duplication of effort.

Data management

- **Contact reports.** Are development officers responsible for inputting their contact reports? Are they responsible for generating and distributing their own progress reports?
- **System reports.** Who will generate and print the reports: your computer staff or your office staff? Will the reports be batched to run at night? Who will design the way information will be laid out in the reports? How and how often should a given report be done (online or on paper, daily or monthly)?
- **Security.** This is paramount. Your moves-management system may have numerous users, all of whom should have specifically defined viewing and editing rights. You need to make sure that the information is secure but also available to the correct personnel. For example, you should permit only the development officer who entered a contact report to change that report. Also, you need to ensure that members of your staff enforce donor confidentiality

Phases of movement

Define all the different phases of movement, including identification, cultivation, solicitation, and stewardship. This may seem insignificant, but all persons who are entering moves information need to be on the same page. Consistent data entry and coding are critical to any information system.

Problem resolution

If two development officers are targeting one donor, who gets the specific responsibility and credit? How do you handle donors who accidentally discover they're on your Top 100 list? These are just two of several problems you need to be prepared to resolve.

EVALUATING AND REVIEWING YOUR SYSTEM

As I mentioned earlier, moves management is resource intensive, so you need to be prepared to measure and defend your system's effectiveness. Are you getting the desired return on your investment? Are you improving the relationship with the prospect? Evaluate all components of your system by asking questions such as these:

- **Planning:** Was the planning sufficient? Did you forget something? Did you properly evaluate or reassign a prospect through the process?
- **Prospect pool:** Did you properly identify a prospect? Did you miss one? Why? Did you have the right information or review process to determine prospects?
- **Information tracking system:** Is the staff actually using it? Is the tracking system easy to use, or is it a hindrance? Is the information helpful? Is there a need for additional training?
- **Staffing and support:** Do you have enough staff? Are you getting the support you need from your staff and higher-ups? Are you fully using staff members, administration, and volunteers?
- **Policies and procedures:** Are they being followed? Do they need to be updated?

As more nonprofits struggle to meet the challenges of cost containment, competition, and limited resources, a moves-management system will help nurture relationships more effectively. With proper teamwork and communication, the system can help your development office become the catalyst, engineer, and champion of increased support.

References

Broce, Thomas E. *Fund Raising: The Guide To Raising Money From Private Sources:* University of Oklahoma Press: Norman and London, 1990. 290 pages.

Dunlop, David R. "Major Gift Fund Raising," CASE Summer Institute (Summer 1993)

Dunlop, David R.. "Strategic Management of a Major Gift Program," CASE conference on Developing an Effective Major Gift Program. 1993.

Gearhart, G. David. *The Capital Campaign in Higher Education: A Practical Guide for College and University Advancement,* National Association of College and University Business Officers. 1995.

Karsch, Carole W. "Prospect Management: Tracking and Coordinating Information," CASE conference on Developing an Effective Major Gift Program. 1993.

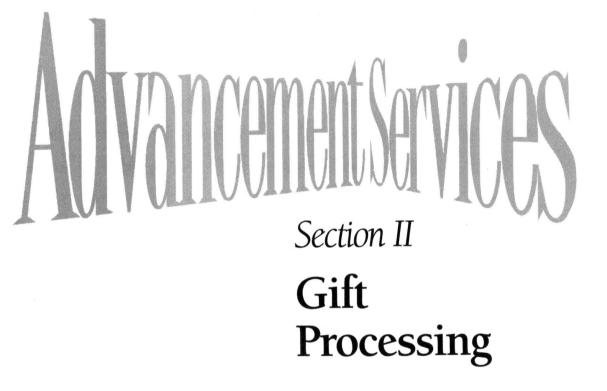

Section II

Gift
Processing

Chapter 5

The Nuts and Bolts of Gift Substantiation

■ By Patricia L. Reynolds
Director of Advancement Services
The Foundation of the State University of New York at
Binghamton

A major prospect has traveled the path from identification to cultivation to solicitation and, at last, has just made a generous gift. Your campus leaders are excitedly making plans to announce and celebrate this largess.

Even so, you as an advancement services officer should know that another task comes first: to acknowledge the gift, properly and immediately. After all, your campus can jeopardize its bond with the donor forever if you handle this phase of the gift process inadequately, inaccurately, or insignificantly.

Donors will and should expect you to acknowledge and document their gifts as soon as possible. These actions not only provide official substantiation for tax and accounting purposes but also solidify the relationship. To handle these important steps properly, you need to understand the different rules for different circumstances. Here is an overview of what you must do to substantiate the most common types of charitable gifts.

SUBSTANTIATION IN BRIEF

According to Internal Revenue Code section 170(f)(8), canceled checks no longer constitute sufficient documentation for the donor to claim a charitable contribution. Instead, the required substantiation may be in the form of a letter, receipt, post card, or other written notification, and must include the following:

- total amount of the cash contribution;
- if a non-cash gift, a description of the item(s), with no value stated;
- a statement as to whether the charity provided the donor any goods or services in exchange for the gift or a portion of the gift; and
- a description and good-faith estimate of the value of any goods or services provided to the donor.

There is no requirement to provide the gift date, and many institutions prefer to acknowledge either the date the gift was received (as we do at Binghamton University) or the date the gift was processed (as is the policy at Duke University). For gifts made by credit card, the IRS considers them received only after the gift is posted to the appropriate account number, so the "date received" and the "date processed" are the same.

For gifts made by credit card, the IRS considers them received only after the gift is posted to the appropriate account number, so the "date received" and the "date processed" are the same.

GIFTS OF $250 OR MORE

The IRS requires all charities to provide a contemporaneous written acknowledgment of each individual cash contribution of $250 or more. In this context, "contemporaneous" means you must send the acknowledgment on or before the date on which the donor files a tax return, or on or before the due date for filing that return, whichever is earlier.

Although the donor is not required to submit this substantiation with the tax form, the regulations clearly state that you, as the charitable organization, must send the receipt or letter before the donor completes his or her form.

GIFTS OF REAL OR PERSONAL PROPERTY

You can acknowledge gifts of real estate or other personal property, including books, art work, and equipment, with a letter containing a description of the items donated and the designated department or program receiving the items. You shouldn't provide a dollar value in the acknowledgment letter, as there are special regulations regarding the value placed on in-kind gifts.

As of January 1, 1985, the IRS required that charitable institutions maintain detailed records on all gifts of property (other than cash and publicly traded securities) with a value greater than $500. Records should contain the location of the property, the purpose of the donation, and information on any subsequent sale of the property. Donors making gifts of property in excess of $500 are required to file IRS Form 8283 reporting such gifts when they file their federal income tax returns. It is the donor's responsibility to obtain and complete Form 8283, which will then require the signature of the authorized official at your institution who received the donated property.

In addition, donors must obtain a qualified written appraisal for each item of affected property with a value greater than $5,000. They may have similar items appraised as a unit. The institution receiving the gift may not obtain or pay for the appraisal, which must be made by an independent appraiser. Donors must also submit the appraisals and Form 8283 to the charitable institution so the designated official can sign the form and retain a copy of the appraisals.

PAYROLL DEDUCTION AND BANK DRAFT GIFTS

Special rules govern contributions made by payroll deduction. The de minimis substantiation requirement does not apply unless the amount withheld from each paycheck is $250 or more. The donor may substantiate payroll deduction contributions with a document specifying the amount being deducted from each paycheck and a statement from the charity stating that no goods or services were provided in whole or partial consideration for payroll deduction contributions. If any goods or services are provided, the payroll deduction substantiation is subject to the same regulations as any other charitable contribution. This is explained more fully in the next section.

Gifts made by bank draft or electronic fund transfer (EFT) are subject to the same rules as gifts made by check or credit card. If the individual amount deducted each time is less than $250, the IRS requires no substantiation. EFT gifts of $250 or more would require the same type of gift substantiation as outlined above.

Several institutions, including Binghamton, provide statements at the end of the calendar year listing total contributions from payroll-deduction and EFT participants, even though this is not required. Other institutions, such as Duke University, will provide end-of-year statements at the donor's request.

QUID PRO QUO CONTRIBUTIONS

A *quid pro quo* is defined as any payment made partly as a gift and partly as a payment for specified goods or services that the charity provides to the donor. Any quid pro quo contribution that exceeds $75 requires a written disclosure for the goods or services provided. The disclosure statement must:

- inform the donor that the tax-deductible portion of the gift is limited to the portion of the gift in excess of the value of the goods or services, and
- include a good-faith estimate of the value of the goods and services provided.

Your institution can make this disclosure either at the time of solicitation or after you've received the gift. Failure to do so carries a penalty. The IRS may impose a $10 fee on you for each contribution that did not receive the appropriate disclosure information, not to exceed $5,000 per fund-raising event or direct mail solicitation.

THE EXCEPTION TO THE QUID PRO QUO RULE

When you give donors goods and services that are defined as having only de minimis value, they aren't required to deduct the value of these premiums from their contributions. The IRS's safe-harbor guidelines published in 1990 permit you to provide small items or benefits of token value without affecting a gift's tax deductibility.

To prevent donors from being subject to the usual quid pro quo rules, you must first inform them about quid pro quo considerations. In addition, you must meet at least one of the following three requirements:

1. The fair market value of all benefits received must exceed neither 2 percent of the total contribution nor the IRS-established ceiling that is adjusted annually for inflation (in 1999: $72).

2. The contribution is at or over the established de minimis level, which is also adjusted annually for inflation (in 1999: $36); the benefits are token items (defined as bookmarks, calendars, key chains, mugs, posters, and T-shirts) that bear the organization's name or logo; and the cost of all benefits received falls within the established limit, also adjusted for inflation (in 1999: $7.20).

> *To prevent donors from being subject to the usual quid pro quo rules, you must first inform them about quid pro quo considerations.*

3. You mail or distribute to donors items satisfying the de minimis limitations outlined above along with a request for a contribution. Donors must not have requested the items. Your solicitations must include a statement indicating that donors may keep the items whether or not they make a contribution.

When you provide goods or services of de minimis value, either your solicitation material or the receipt/acknowledgment should include a statement similar to the following:

"Under Internal Revenue Service guidelines, the estimated value of [the benefits received] is not substantial; therefore, the full amount of your contribution is tax deductible as allowed by law."

For more on this subject, see Chapter 6.

MEMBERSHIP BENEFITS

Many charities, such as museums, libraries, and zoos, use membership packages to build a base of support. Benefits typically include free parking, use of facilities, and invitations to lectures or tours. At Binghamton University, the Friends of the Library and Friends of the Greenhouse are membership organiza-

How Do Others Handle Gift Substantiation?

Procedures for processing gifts and providing proper substantiation differ from institution to institution. Even so, knowing how others work can help you find the right process for you. Here's a quick look at a few campuses' routines.

At Binghamton, which is one of the four University Centers in the State University of New York system, each gift is acknowledged within 48 hours by a computer-generated receipt that contains all required information in compliance with IRS regulations. The advancement services office sends this official receipt.

However, some contributions get further attention. Gifts at the $1,000 level and above also receive a personal letter that the director of donor relations prepares for either the foundation president or the university president to sign, depending on the amount of the gift. Deans, program directors, development officers, and others who have a special relationship with the donor may also send a personal note of appreciation.

At the University of North Carolina at Chapel Hill, computer-generated receipts for cash and credit card gifts go out within 24 hours. Stock letters are prepared individually and sent out as soon as the valuation is available and designation of the gift is known. The stewardship office prepares personal letters for gifts of $2,000 or more for the Chancellor's signature. The schools and units are encouraged to prepare letters for their donors, but they do not have to cover the business aspects of the gifts.

At Western Michigan University, all gifts receive a computer-generated acknowledgment letter processed by development staff and signed by the president of the WMU Foundation. If appropriate, the computer letter is replaced with a personalized letter drafted by the development secretary and signed by the president of the foundation. All gifts receive computer-generated tax receipts processed by the gift accounting staff and computer-signed by the treasurer of the WMU Foundation. Gifts of $5,000 and more receive a computer-generated acknowledgment letter processed by donor relations staff and signed by the president of the university. If appropriate, a personalized letter drafted by donor relations staff and signed by the university president replaces a computer letter.

The University of Idaho uses a slightly different approach. It mails each receipt inside a pre-printed, formal acknowledgment card. The message on the card varies according to the size of the gift. In addition, gifts over a specific dollar amount receive a personalized letter from the president.

As you've read, IRS regulations require that the acknowledgment contain a statement indicating that no goods or services were provided in exchange for all or part of the cash or property contributed. At Binghamton, we print this statement on the front of the receipt. Duke University also prints this statement on the front of the receipt and, in addition, provides the donor with further explanation of the IRS regulation by printing a disclaimer about any benefits provided on the back of the receipt.

If your institution did provide the donor with any goods or services, your acknowledgment must contain a description and good-faith estimate of the value of those goods or services, along with an indication of the portion of the gift that is tax deductible. You can include this information on the receipt, as we at Binghamton do, or in a separate statement. At UNC-Chapel Hill, for example, the individual unit that receives the gift is responsible for notifying the donor as to the part of the gift that is not tax deductible. IRS rules indicate that you can also make this disclosure when your fund raiser is soliciting the gift. But the amount that is tax deductible is what should appear on the receipt or in the letter.

tions that solicit support annually.

There are two types of membership benefits that, when offered in exchange for a payment of $75 or less, definitely do not qualify as goods or services that will affect the contribution's tax deductibility:

1. Free admission to members-only events that cost the charity little or nothing—that is, that are no higher than the low-cost limit ($7.20 for 1999). Such events would include lectures and small receptions.
2. Rights or privileges that members can exercise frequently during the membership period (such as library privileges). This excludes any rights to purchase tickets for athletic events.

The IRS doesn't consider member newsletters or program guides to have a measurable value if the publications are not of "commercial quality" (such as a professional journal or a publication containing advertising). Such publications must be provided to members only and unavailable to nonmembers by paid subscription or on the newsstand. The publication's primary purpose must be restricted to informing members about the group's activities.

Note that this "safe harbor" for membership benefits applies only to *frequently available benefits*. For example, for a museum or library that donors can use often and whenever they choose, free parking or free admission is considered to have insubstantial value. However, a benefit that provides an admission discount to scheduled performances or athletic events cannot be *frequently* exercised because the benefit is limited by an established schedule. Therefore, such a benefit would not meet the requirements of the IRS safe-harbor regulations, and the value of the gift would be reduced by the value of the benefit. Again, you should disclose this information to donors at the time you invite them to become members or when you acknowledge their membership payment.

GIFTS OF SECURITIES

Contributions of privately owned securities require a special form of written substantiation that provides the donor with the actual date of transfer, the number of shares transferred, and the average per share value of the stock or bond as of the date of transfer. [For more details about this, see Chapter 7.]

In addition, you must again include a statement to indicate that no goods or services were provided in exchange for the gift. If the donor did receive something other than a de minimis or token benefit, you must state the fair market value of that benefit with an indication of the final tax-deductible portion of the contribution. Gifts of closely held stock in excess of $10,000 also require that the donor complete IRS Form 8283 and obtain the signature of the designated official at the charity that received the donation.

SUBSTANTIATION FOR TRUSTS AND POOLED INCOME FUNDS

The IRS regulations have been modified to provide that the substantiation requirements do not apply to charitable remainder trusts or charitable lead trusts. However, in the case of a transfer of cash or other property to a pooled income fund, you must provide a contemporaneous written acknowledgment stating that the cash or other property was transferred to the fund. And, of course, this substantiation must include a statement indicating whether any goods or services were provided as a result of this transfer, including any income interest provided to the donor.

A VITAL TOOL: CLEAR POLICIES

As you ponder these substantiation rules, think about whether your standard policies cover them adequately—if at all. If not, join the many institutions that are developing written policies and procedures for gift acknowledgment and donor recognition.

Get started by meeting with other staff members who are responsible for gift processing and donor relations. Depending on your institution's size, a standard donor recognition policy may not be enough to address all types of gifts and coordinate decentralized acknowledgment and stewardship activities. Therefore, include all appropriate staff so you can incorporate any special procedures your far-flung departments and offices may use.

Providing proper substantiation in compliance with IRS regulations should be a major objective of any written policy. In addition, your policies should support your institution's mission and reflect your development and alumni programs' philosophy. If you need examples to get started, remember that your colleagues at other schools, colleges, and universities may be willing to share. A number of campuses even post their policies on the Internet for reference.

A small note: An important part of any donor recognition policy addresses the issue of anonymity. Donors who wish to remain anonymous must receive special treatment to ensure that you thank them properly and send them all required substantiation documents while still maintaining their privacy.

Once you've written your policies, the appropriate administrators and board members should approve and endorse them. Then you should distribute them to everyone concerned with building lasting relationships with your donors. Carefully drafted, widely circulated substantiation and acknowledgment policies can help you do so most effectively.

> *Providing proper substantiation in compliance with IRS regulations should be a major objective of any written policy.*

References

Burnett, Jefferson and Donna M. Orem. *Questions and Answers on Gift Substantiation and Quid Pro Quo Disclosure Statement Requirements for Private Schools.* Washington, DC: CASE, National Association of Independent Schools, and the United States Catholic Conference, 1994. 40 pages.

Daily, Linda. "On the Block: Organizers of Auctions and Other Fund-Raising Events Tell How They Work Smart and Stay Legal," CURRENTS 21, no. 4 (April 1995): 22-27.

Dessoff, Alan L. "Put It in Writing," CURRENTS, Vol. 23, No. 3 (February 1997): 30-34.

Federal Register. *Rules and Regulations,* Vol. 61, No. 242 (December 16, 1996): 65946-65955.

McNamee, Mike. "Such a Deal: The New Tax Laws Swap Tougher Receipt Rules for Relief from the Hated AMT," CURRENTS 20, no. 3 (March 1994): 31-33.

Ryan, Ellen. "Common Bonds: Three Experts Offer Tried-and-True Tenets of International Fund Raising," CURRENTS 20, no. 8 (September 1994): 18-22.

Taylor, John H. "The New Marching Orders: Revised Reporting Standards for Annual Giving Take Effect the July. Here's a Quick Guide for Those in the Trenches," CURRENTS 23, no. 2 (February 1997): 36-37.

Taylor, John H. "Your Noncash Gift Questions Answered: Troubled by Stock Gifts, Auctions, Or Gifts in Kind? Here's a Handy Q-and-A Guide to Some of the Most Common Problems of Gift Credit, Value, and Acknowledgment," CURRENTS 24, no. 7 (July/August 1998): 46-52.

Teitell, Conrad. *Planned Giving: Starting, Marketing, Administering.* Old Greenwich, CT: Taxwise Giving, 1996.

Teitell, Conrad. *Teitell's Substantiating Charitable Gifts: The Compleat Compliance Manual.* Old Greenwich, CT: Taxwise Giving, 1995. 637 pages.

Chapter 6

Tax Rules and Regulations: How the IRS Views Deductibility, Qualified Donees, and Usable Receipts

■ By Alison Paul
Attorney
Montana Legal Services Association

Nearly every Section 501(c)(3) organization in the United States conducts fund-raising activities of some form or another. These range from seeking small gifts via direct mail to sponsoring fund-raising banquets to soliciting large donations through a complex planned giving program. To conduct such activities successfully, you as a development professional need to understand the regulations a Section 501(c)(3) organization must follow, both to protect the tax-deductible nature of the donations and to shield itself and its donors from various IRS penalties.

This chapter will help you make sense of the basic IRS rules regarding exactly what makes an individual or corporate gift a tax-deductible charitable contribution. For income tax purposes, the three key aspects of a charitable contribution are:

- **The contribution itself,** since only certain types of donations qualify as tax-deductible charitable contributions.
- **The donee,** because a tax-deductible charitable contribution must be made to a qualified donee, or recipient organization.
- **The receipt,** since the donor must be able to substantiate the charitable contribution as required by the IRS.

THE CONTRIBUTION

For a charitable gift to be considered a "contribution" for income tax purposes, the gift must involve the transfer of money or property to a qualified charitable organization. Gifts of cash or stock are obvious examples of the types of gifts that qualify as tax-deductible charitable contributions.

If you work for an organization that receives only cash gifts, you can stop reading here and skip to the next section.

If you work for an organization that receives only cash gifts, you can stop reading here and skip to the next section. If you're not that lucky, however, it's important to be able to identify what types of transfers to charity fail to qualify as tax-deductible charitable contributions. A fund raiser who inadvertently gives a donor incorrect information about tax deductibility risks bringing down the IRS's wrath upon both the charitable organization and the donor who claimed an inaccurate deduction.

The following list identifies common types of contributions that *do not qualify* as tax-deductible charitable contributions.

- **A payment for a raffle ticket.**
- **A payment earmarked for an individual.** This is not a charitable gift for income tax purposes regardless of the charitable nature of the payment.
- **Volunteer time in service to a charitable organization.** For example, an attorney who gives your organization pro bono legal advice may not take a charitable deduction for the billable value of his or her time. Just to confuse things, however, a volunteer may deduct out-of-pocket expenses, such as mileage, parking, or supplies.
- **A payment earmarked for a charity's lobbying activities.**
- **A gift that is conditional on a future event.** For instance, if

a couple gives a painting to a university but keeps it at home for three months before moving it to campus, the gift is not official until the painting is actually transferred to the university. Another example occurs when donors transfer stock to a charitable organization but retain voting rights over the stock until the end of the year. The gift is not complete until the charitable organization has total control and ownership of the stock.

- **The use of a donor's property by a charitable organization.** For example, if a donor allows a charity to use office space without paying rent, the donor is not allowed to deduct the fair market value of the rent as a contribution to the charity.
- **A quid pro quo contribution.** If donors receive something in exchange for their contributions, then only part of the amount paid is tax deductible. The most common example is a fund-raising dinner; in return for contributions, donors receive the right to attend a fancy (or even not so fancy) social event. The only part of this "contribution" that the IRS considers tax deductible is the excess amount paid over the fair market value of attending the event.

Another example of a quid pro quo contribution is a payment for an item at a charitable auction. (The disclosure requirements imposed on charities with respect to quid pro quo contributions are discussed below.)

Under certain circumstances, when donors receive only a small item or a benefit of token value, the entire amount of the contribution is fully deductible. A benefit is considered a token if:

1. the payment occurs in the context of a fund-raising campaign in which the charity informs contributors what amount constitutes a deductible contribution; and

2. the fair market value of the benefits received is not more than 2 percent of the payment or $72, whichever is less; or the payment is $36 or more and the only benefits received are token items bearing the organization's name (such as a mug or T-shirt).

The cost (not fair market value) of all of the items received must be less than $7.20. (These amounts, which are current for 1999 donations, are adjusted for inflation each year; the IRS announces the updated amounts every December.)

- **Certain parts of a payment by a donor for the right to purchase tickets to athletic events.** Under IRS regulations, 80 percent of such a payment is treated as a charitable contribution and 20 percent as a payment for the right to purchase the tickets. For example, if a donor pays a university $300 for the right to purchase basketball tickets, the substantiation receipt the university furnishes must show that the taxpayer received a benefit of $60 for the right to purchase the tickets. The taxpayer may then treat $240 as a deductible charitable contribution.
- **A corporation's contribution to a foreign organization.** However, when a corporation contributes funds to a charitable corporation organized in the United States and the funds are to be used abroad, the gift is tax deductible as a charitable contribution. (For this rule to apply, the charitable organization donee must be formally organized as a corporation, not another type of legal entity, such as a trust.)
- **Payment to a charity for publishing or otherwise publicizing a gift acknowledgment that includes an endorsement or other comparative language concerning a donor's products or services.** In a case like this, the payment is considered not a charitable contribution but rather a payment for advertising.

However, under IRS regulations effective December 31, 1997, if a corporation's payment qualifies as a "qualified corporate sponsorship payment," the IRS will consider it a charitable contribution. To qualify for a deduction, the corporate contributor can receive an acknowledgment of the contribution from the charity. But any further language will be considered advertising. To comply with this regulation, a charity may divide a single payment by a corporate sponsor between a qualified sponsorship payment and a payment for advertising services.

Clearly, IRS regulations about deductibility are many and varied. But still other issues come into play in this realm as well.

The last one we'll cover here is the question of when the charitable gift occurs. Although this seems easy, determining when a charitable gift takes place can actually become quite complicated because of the many different forms a gift can take. The basic rule is that a charitable gift is complete at such time as the charity receives the cash or property. However, the IRS has stated that a charitable gift made by check is complete at the time the check is delivered or mailed, provided the bank eventually honors the check. For example, a check mailed on December 30, 1999, would be considered a 1999 charitable contribution even though the charity did not receive the check and the funds did not clear the bank until January 2000.

A gift of securities or stock is made at the time the certificate is delivered or mailed to the charity with a transferring document, such as a signed stock power. If a stockbroker completes the transaction, the gift is considered to be made when the stocks are re-registered in the charity's name. Accordingly, if a charity receives a letter stating that the donor has transferred 50 shares of stock to a charity on December 29 of one year, but the securities are not actually re-registered until February of the next year, the transfer did not actually occur until the second year.

> *If you work for an independent school, college, university, or other established charity, it's unlikely that you need to be concerned about proving your organization is a qualified donee.*

THE DONEE

As a development professional soliciting donations from individuals or corporations, you need to understand which organizations the IRS considers "qualified donees." If you work for an independent school, college, university, or other established charity, it's unlikely that you need to be concerned about proving your organization is a qualified donee. However, let's say you have to address the deductibility of contributions to other related organizations, such as independent auxiliaries, some of your charitable organization's programs, or payments under a matching gift program your organization operates. In such cases, it's important to understand which organizations the IRS considers qualified donees.

An individual or corporation may deduct contributions to organizations described in Internal Revenue Code Section 170(c). For practical purposes, most organizations described in Internal Revenue Code Section 501(c)(3) will also qualify under Internal Revenue Code Section 170(c). In addition, organizations like hospitals, universities, and churches generally qualify to receive tax-deductible charitable contributions under Internal Revenue Code Section 170, regardless of their status as Section 501(c)(3) organizations.

But other types of tax-exempt organizations are not recognized recipients of tax-deductible charitable contributions. For example, the IRS does not allow deductions under Section 170(c) for contributions to social welfare organizations exempt under Section 501(c)(4), for business leagues exempt under Section 501(c)(6), and for social clubs exempt under Section 501(c)(7).

To be described in section 501(c)(3) of the Internal Revenue Code, an organization must be organized and operated exclusively for religious, charitable, scientific, literary, or educational purposes. No part of its net earnings may inure to the benefit of any private individual. No substantial part of its activities may carry on propaganda or otherwise attempt to influence legislation. And the organization may not intervene or participate in any campaign on behalf of or in opposition to any candidate for public office. Every charitable organization described in Section 501(c)(3) is presumed to be a private foundation unless it establishes otherwise to the satisfaction of the IRS. However, whether a Section 501(c)(3) organization is considered a public charity or a private foundation is only important if the contribution is to be made by a private foundation. Individual and corporate donors can make tax-deductible charitable contributions to either type of organization.

> *To be described in section 501(c)(3) of the Internal Revenue Code, an organization must be organized and operated exclusively for religious, charitable, scientific, literary, or educational purposes.*

Verification of a donee's tax-exempt status

A donor may want verification that your organization is a qualified donee. The most reliable way to verify tax status is to give the donor a copy of your organization's IRS determination letter. This letter will state the type of 501(c) organization and, if the organization is a 501(c)(3), whether it's a private foundation or a public charity. If this letter is more than five years old (as it often is), a donor may also request a signed statement that there have been no material changes in your organization's tax status since the letter was issued.

If an organization is unable to find its IRS determination letter, the organization can always write to the IRS for confirmation or verification that it is a Section 501(c)(3) organization and then get a copy of the IRS's letter.

You should be aware that hospitals, universities, and other educational institutions may not have a determination letter from the IRS since they are not required to apply for Section 501(c)(3) status. Accordingly, many donors will not require verification of the tax status of these types of organizations. If they do require it, a corporate officer of the organization may verify by signed statement that the organization is qualified to receive tax-deductible contributions under Internal Revenue Code Section 170(c).

The second most reliable way to demonstrate your organization's tax status is to confirm that it is listed in IRS Publication 78 (the renowned *Cumulative List*). The IRS updates this publication annually (as of October 31) and lists organizations to which gifts are deductible for income tax purposes. Between updates of the list, revocation of tax-exempt status is published weekly in the *Internal Revenue Bulletin*.

You may obtain IRS Publication 78 from the Superintendent of Documents, U.S. Government Printing Office, Washington, DC, 20402. (Just ask for Publication 78.) In addition, for the electronically literate, the publication is available at the IRS' World Wide Web site at *www.irs.ustreas.gov/plain/bus_info/eo/index. htm* (plain text format). This is a rather unwieldy, yet searchable, database that purports to list (and to allow your most probing donors to find) all organizations covered by Publication 78.

THE RECEIPT

Several years ago, the IRS adopted a set of requirements for documenting tax-deductible charitable contributions. These rules govern the type of documentation an individual or corporation must keep to substantiate a gift to a charitable organization. In fact, if an individual makes a charitable contribution of more than $250 to an organization, that person may not claim a tax deduction for the contribution unless he or she has the required receipt by the time the tax return is filed.

It can be difficult to square IRS rules with your standard donor recognition practices. It's all too easy to issue a thank-you letter that is beautifully worded yet fails to contain the "magic" language the IRS requires. While the donor may appreciate your eloquence, the person is unlikely to make another gift if your oversight means that he or she is not able to deduct the charitable contribution.

So what should an individual or corporation use as docu-

Suggested Language for Acknowledging a Charitable Gift

Thank you for your contribution on *[insert date]* of [insert amount of cash contribution or description of property. If this is a gift of property, do not value the property].

[Then use one of the following statements:]

We estimate that the fair market value of the *[describe goods or services]* you have received from *[name of the organization that provided a benefit to the donor]* is $*[insert FMV]*. The amount of your contribution that is deductible as a charitable contribution for federal income tax purposes is $*[insert deductible amount]* (the excess of the amount of your contribution over the value of the goods or services we provided to you).

[Or]

As no goods or services were provided to you in return for your charitable contribution, the entire amount of your contribution is tax deductible to the full extent otherwise allowed by law.

mentation to prove that a gift is a deductible contribution? If a contribution is $250 or more, the individual or corporation is required to obtain a receipt with these three features:

- a statement that the charity received the contribution,
- the amount of the contribution or a description of the property that was contributed, and
- a statement regarding whether or not any goods or services were received by the donor in exchange for the contribution.

At left is an example of language that you may use to meet this requirement. While you are not required to use this exact language, each part must nevertheless appear in your thank-you letter.

Note that under IRS rules, it is critical that the gift acknowledgment indicates whether the donor received goods or services in return for the gift. An individual authorized by the organization to issue tax receipts should sign the receipt. Donors must have the receipt by the time they file a tax return for the year in which the gift was made (including any extensions).

If your organization is lucky enough to receive contributions in excess of $10,000 in the form of cash, foreign currency, cashier's checks, money orders, bank drafts, or traveler's checks, you must file IRS Form 8300. This form requires you to report the amount and method of payment, to describe the transaction (i.e., whether it's an unrestricted charitable contribution or other type of transfer), and to verify the donor's identity. You may verify by examining a document that's normally accepted for identification, such as a driver's license, passport, or other official document. You must provide the donor with a copy of Form 8300 as filed with the IRS.

DISCLOSURE REQUIREMENTS IMPOSED ON CHARITIES

The IRS requires *donors* to obtain receipts that include the three elements listed above. In the interests of good donor relations, most charities are careful to ensure that their receipts include all the required information.

However, under certain circumstances, the IRS imposes a burden to disclose on the charitable recipient. If a donor pays more than $75 to a charity and the charity provides any goods or services to the donor in exchange for the gift, the charity must provide a written disclosure statement to the donor. It should state that the amount of the deductible contribution is limited to the excess of the amount contributed by the donor over the value of the goods or services the charity provided to the donor. Furthermore, the statement must include a good-faith estimate of the fair market value of the goods or services the donor received. The charity is not required to value the donor's contribution.

SUBSTANTIATION OF GIFTS FROM PRIVATE FOUNDATIONS

If you're a development officer for a nonprofit, you are likely to be soliciting gifts from private foundations. A foundation is not required to substantiate gifts to donees under the substantiation rules discussed above. Because a foundation does not pay income tax, it is not required to prove that its contributions are tax deductible.

Instead, a different set of rules applies. A foundation must prove that any distribution by the foundation is a qualified distribution for purposes of complying with the foundation tax rules. At minimum, the foundation will want to verify that the donee you represent is a Section 501(c)(3) organization and a public charity. A foundation may ask for a copy of your organization's determination letter from the IRS showing that it is described in Section 501(c)(3) and qualifies as a public charity. In addition, for particularly large grants, a foundation may require a signed copy of the grant letter and program information about your charitable organization, such as a copy of your latest budget, annual report, or most recent tax return.

SUBSTANTIATION OF NON-CASH CONTRIBUTIONS

Increasingly, donors are willing to donate property as opposed to solely making cash gifts. Accordingly, it is important to understand how the IRS expects these donations to be valued and reported. There is potential for abuse by donors who overvalue property to reduce the amount of tax they must pay to the government. To keep track of property that is donated to charities, the IRS requires the donor, the tax-exempt organization, or both to submit a series of reporting forms. Following is a discussion of the two forms that can affect the charity receiving a noncash donation.

- **Form 8283.** An individual or corporate donor must file Form 8283 if the amount of the donor's deduction for all noncash gifts made to charitable organizations is greater than $500. The primary function of Form 8283 is for the donor to set forth the value of the donated property for which the deduction is claimed and for the charitable organization to acknowledge receipt of the gift.

If your organization receives property for which the donor is claiming a charitable deduction in excess of $5,000, your organization's name, address, and employer identification number must be included on the Form 8283. In addition, an authorized official of your organization must acknowledge the gift and state that it will file Form 8282 in the event that the organization sells, exchanges, or otherwise disposes of the donated property within two years after the date when your organization receives the property. The person acknowledging the gift to the charity must be an official authorized to sign the organization's tax returns or a person specifically designated to sign Form 8283. Note that a person in the organization's development office is not likely to qualify as an authorized individual unless an officer or the board of directors has specifically designated that individual to sign.

By signing the donor's Form 8283, the Section 501(c)(3) organization is not indicating that it agrees with the claimed fair market value of the donated property. Therefore, simply signing the form should not make your organi-

If your organization receives property for which the donor is claiming a charitable deduction in excess of $5,000, your organization's name, address, and employer identification number must be included on the Form 8283.

zation liable for overvaluing the property. The donor is required to furnish you with a copy of the signed Form 8283.

- **Form 8282.** If your organization disposes of property for which it signed a Form 8283 within two years after receiving a contribution, you are required to file Form 8282 with the IRS. There are, however, two important exceptions in which Form 8282 does not need to be filed.

1. If the original donee provided on its appraisal summary a statement that the appraised value of a donated item was not more than $500 at the time of the contribution; and

2. If the property the charitable organization received is consumed or distributed without consideration, in fulfilling its charitable purpose or function.

In all other cases, Form 8282 must be filed within 125 days after the date your organization disposes of the property, and a copy of the form must be provided to the original donor.

It is important to note that the requirement to file Form 8282 applies to successor donee organizations if the property is transferred to another charitable organization. If you fail to file Form 8282, fail to include all of the required information, or include incorrect information on the form, you may be subject to IRS penalties. The penalty for each violation is generally $50, with an annual limit not to exceed $250,000.

Chapter 7

Accepting, Valuing, and Acknowledging Gifts of Securities

■ By Pamela Todd Fox
Director of Development Resources
Allegheny College

After meeting with Bob from your development office, Ima Donor decides to give some of her highly appreciated stock to establish a pooled income fund at her alma mater, National College. Because the stock market is bullish, Bob recommends that she contact her broker as soon as possible. Ima writes a letter instructing her broker to transfer a specific number of shares to National College, but just to make sure the timing is right, she also calls her broker to initiate the transaction. He calls you in advancement services.

Now what? A gift of appreciated securities is one of the best ways donors can support a charitable institution. Whether they're given as part of an annual or capital program, and whether they're an outright gift or a life income gift, securities are the most common form of noncash or property gifts. Donors like to give securities for several reasons. They're easy to give; they're often highly appreciated above cost basis, thus providing tax advantages; and they're often easier to part with than outright cash.

As an advancement services officer, your role is to facilitate the process. When brokers call your office to effect a transfer of securities, it is imperative that they receive clear instructions in an efficient manner. The value of the gift depends on the timing of the gift. If the stock market is dropping, a broker needs to process the transfer of assets so that the value of the stock is preserved and the donors' intended gift amount is realized. If the market is rising, you will want to effect the transfer as quickly as possible to benefit from the gift's increased value.

In this chapter, we'll explore several aspects of creating an effective process for accepting gifts of securities, from establishing a routine to valuing gifts. On page 74, you can also read about how to handle four typical cases, including Ima's.

THE CASE FOR CENTRALIZED AUTHORITY

G iving securities is an easy way to contribute to an institution, especially if one person oversees such transactions. Who that overseer is can vary from campus to campus. Often it's the treasurer, since the treasurer's office is also empowered to liquidate or re-invest these assets. But it could be the planned giving director or major gifts officer, since one of them probably facilitated the gift. Or it may be advancement services, since gift recording is involved.

As I see it, the process will work most smoothly if the development office has clear authority over gift acceptance. Such centralized authority is desirable for a number of reasons:

- The donor or broker who alerts the institution will be assisted quickly and efficiently. Again, this is important because valuation of the gift depends upon timing as the stock market fluctuates day by day.
- Each donor and each transaction will be handled consistently.
- When several stock gifts come into your institution at once, especially at calendar-year (or tax-year) end, one designated person can monitor stock transactions more effectively.

CREATING A STOCK-ACCEPTANCE FORM

Having standard paperwork available will do much to make accepting securities easy for both your donors and your campus. You can create a stock-acceptance form in word-processing software or a spreadsheet. The minimum information required for gift recording and documentation is:

- donor name and system ID number;
- gift date (which may not be the same as the processing date);
- stock name and symbol, and number of shares;
- price per share, high of the gift date;
- price per share, low of the gift date
- mean price per share; and
- gift designation.

You must attach all documents attending the transaction to your stock-acceptance form. These documents can include the envelopes the stocks and powers were delivered in (more later on that subject); notes; newspaper documentation for valuation purposes; correspondence; and mathematical computations. As a courtesy, you should also send notification to the development officer responsible for bringing in this gift if you know who the officer is.

VALUING GIFTS OF SECURITIES

What is a gift of stock worth?
You can't determine that until you determine the date of gift, which depends upon the method of transfer. [For more about possible methods, see the case studies on page 74.] The donor's gift value is set by the value on the day your institution receives it—not by the sale price when the institution decides to liquidate the asset.

Most stocks that are given as gifts are traded regularly on a national market such as the New York Stock Exchange, the American Stock Exchange, or the NASDAQ, or on a regional exchange. Most of these exchanges list traded stocks in the *Wall Street Journal* or other major newspapers. You can also go to such Web sites as *www.tradepbs.com/pbscgi/hstgtetol* or *www.financialweb.com/stocktools/*. Since you probably will not know what exchange a particular security is listed under, you can refer to *Standard & Poor's Register of Corporations, Volume 1*. This alphabetical listing of thousands of corporations will present each exchange a stock is traded on.

To get started on valuing a security, use the newspaper published the first business day after the date of gift. Locate the stock exchange and symbol of the stock the company issue is traded under. The stocks are listed by symbol, a one- to four-letter code representing the company. For example, Household International Incorporated is HI. If you don't know the company's symbol, call the company (the *S&P Register* will list a headquarters phone number), or find its homepage on the Internet.

In the newspaper financial or market section, you will find stock exchange listings. Following down the left-hand column of the listing, locate the stock symbol that seems the best fit. The listing will look something like this:

52 Weeks					Yld		Vol				Net
Hi	Lo	Stock	Sym	Div	%	PE	100s	Hi	Lo	Close	Chg
$53^5/8$	23	HshldInt	HI	.60	1.9	41	234893	$3^3/8$	$31^1/8$	$31^3/4$	- 1

The first Hi and Lo figures are averages for the previous 52 weeks. You'll use the second set of Hi and Lo figures to determine the value of the security on the date of the gift. Add these two figures together and divide by 2. The resulting figure is the mean value of the security, used to determine the value of the gift.

To value 100 shares of Household International, convert the fractions to decimals and proceed as follows:

(Hi + Lo) / 2 = Mean Value of Shares

Mean Value of Shares x Number of Shares = Value of Gift

Or:

(33.375 + 31.125) / 2 = 64.50 / 2 = 32.25 = Mean Value

32.25 x 100 shares = 3,225

For a total gift value of $3,225.

If you cannot locate the correct symbol, do not guess. You may be looking under the wrong stock exchange, the company may be listed under a different name, or the stock may not have traded on that day.

Establishing value can be tricky. Here are some potential problems:

ACCEPTING, VALUING, AND ACKNOWLEDGING GIFTS OF SECURITIES

- **No sales on gift date.** If the stock was not traded on the day of the gift valuation, but there was trading activity before and after the date of gift, the calculation for value is found by averaging the mean value on the nearest dates before and after gift date. In other words, look over the reports for the previous five business days and find the activity on the closest date before the gift. Wait the same number of days after the gift date. Average both days' high and low figures. Add the two mean values together and divide by two to get the figure for valuation purposes.
- **Unlisted securities.** For various reasons, some securities are not listed regularly but are traded. To obtain quotes for valuation, you must contact a broker or the issuing company.
- **Closely held stock.** Privately owned corporate stock is difficult to value because it's not traded on a market where its price can be assessed on a regular basis. Its value must be calculated based on factors prescribed by IRS regulations, such as the condition of the company, its market share and position, and the value of similar businesses whose stocks are publicly traded. If the gift is in excess of $10,000, you will need to obtain a qualified appraisal. Refer such gifts to an expert.

> *To get started on valuing a security, use the newspaper published the first business day after the date of gift.*

ACKNOWLEDGING GIFTS OF SECURITIES

When valuing a stock gift, you are using information from a third party, checking a newspaper, and using your own judgment and skills. All are subject to error.

To protect the donor, suggest that the figures be checked for tax purposes. The letter should acknowledge the high and low figures for the trading day and can include the value the institution calculated. To protect both donor and institution, it would be useful to have a disclaimer such as "The figures calculated by National College are believed to be as accurate as possible. Please check with your financial advisers."

For gifts in excess of $500, be sure to include a Form 8283 for the donor's convenience. You or the donor may also get these forms from the bank. In any case, the institution's financial officer must sign the form.

THE PAYOFF

Obviously, securities require plenty of time and attention. But getting the process right is worth all the work. If your institution fails to handle the process well, many brokers will discourage their clients from making such gifts. But brokers who are handled with respect, efficiency, and clear instructions will remember how easy you made this gift. We at Allegheny College

---

Four Case Studies in Accepting and Valuing Gifts of Securities

Scenario No. 1: Ima calls her broker and instructs him to transfer shares to your campus's account.

What happens next depends on whether you and Ima share the same brokerage. If you do, she may transfer certificates into your institutional account quickly and simply. All you need to give the broker is the account number. Usually the transaction is completed on the same day, which is the effective gift date used for valuing the security.

If you do not share the same brokerage, your campus may wish to set up an institutional account with Ima's broker. To do so, you must clear this with your financial office, which generally has the authority to set up such accounts, and then provide the broker with your tax ID number, name, and authorization. After the account is established, usually within a day or two of the request, the broker simply moves the securities into your account. This gift is completed when the shares enter your account, not on the day of instructions. So you use the date of completion for valuing the stock gift.

If your institution does not have an account with the donor's broker and doesn't wish to open one, there are two other options for transferring stock. The broker may use the Depository Trust Company (DTC), a clearinghouse for security transactions, to transfer the shares into your institutional account (see Scenario #3) or re-register the stock to the institution (see Scenario #4).

Scenario No. 2: Harold, who keeps all his stock certificates in a safe-deposit box at his local bank, wants to give physical certificates.

This is actually a risky method of transfer. Once the owner has signed a certificate on the back, it is negotiable and legal tender. Anyone may liquidate it.

So instead, you should encourage Harold to use a much safer method of delivery: a stock power. It's a form that, when signed by the owner and filled out by the institutional broker, effectively transfers the shares.

Each physical stock certificate a donor decides to send to your institution must have a stock power. You may send the stock powers to the donor, or you or the donor may be able to get them at the bank. In any case, the donor must sign the stock power exactly as the name appears on the stock. If the stock is in joint names, then both parties must sign the stock power exactly as their names appear on the stock. A bank officer must guarantee the signature(s), so it's best that donors actually go to the bank prior to signing the stock power. Donors should not fill out the rest of the stock power; the institutional broker will complete the form.

Once Harold makes his intention known to you, instruct him to send the unendorsed physical certificate to your attention in one envelope and the signed stock power in a separate envelope. Because the stock power transferring the

have had many brokers recommend us for gifts from donors whom we were not aware owned stock.

Prospects who find your process easy to follow will be security donors again and again. If they feel good about their experience with your institution, you will, too.

A final note about gifts of securities: As easy as they are to give, they are subject to rather strict tax laws and can be thorny to deal with. Your institution is required to have clear and legal

---

shares to your institution is in a separate envelope from the actual certificate, they are safe from theft. When the stock and power are received, the stock is negotiable.

What about valuation? Stock gifts received through the mail are valued based upon the most recent postmark date on the envelope. The gift is not complete until both the certificate and the power are received at your institution. Be sure to keep both envelopes.

Of course, Harold could just walk the stock certificate and the stock power form over to the advancement offices if he wanted to. In that case, the gift date would be the date when he hand-delivered them to your institution.

Scenario No. 3: Frank's broker wants to transfer via the Depository Trust Company (DTC).

Physical stock certificates are becoming a thing of the past simply because most securities are stored and tracked electronically. It may be easier for both the donor's broker and your institution to accept security transfers through the Depository Trust Company, possibly the safest and fastest method of transferring stocks.

Your institutional broker will have a DTC account, the ID for which consists of two series of numbers. When the donor's broker contacts you for instructions, you give him your DTC account numbers. The securities are then electronically transmitted from the brokerage DTC account into your institution's DTC account. This transaction normally takes one to five days to complete.

Sometimes a donor's broker who has your institutional DTC numbers will act upon a transaction without notifying your institution. This can cause a delay in receipt of the gift and consequently a delay in acknowledging your donor's generosity. Through your literature and in conversation with brokers, be sure to emphasize the importance of notifying the institution of such gifts before they happen.

The date the securities hit your DTC account is the effective date of receipt and thus the date used for valuing the gift. In all instances of electronic transfer, you must require from the donor a letter of instruction to validate the transfer.

Scenario No. 4: Prudence instructs the company to re-register ownership of her shares to your institution.

This is the least effective method of transferring shares to a charitable institution because it's slow; it can take upwards of six weeks to complete this transaction. In this instance, Prudence may instruct either the company or the broker to re-register the stock. The company will re-issue a certificate in your organization's name and send the re-registered stock to you. The date of issue determines the date of gift.

Occasionally, a donor will want to give only part of the total shares on the certificate. In this case, the stock must be re-registered with the company. The donors must write a letter to the company instructing it to split the certificate, re-registering a portion to the institution and retaining a portion of the stock for themselves.

title of transfer in all instances; hence the stock power form. In addition, you must provide a substantiated date of gift and valuation of the gift; remember the postmarked envelope you kept and the letter you asked for from the donor?

Beyond these basics, don't assume responsibility for being the last word on how to accept securities. Tax laws, and their implications, are best left to the tax accountants and advisers.

References

"Valuation of Charitable Gifts," In *Tax Economics of Charitable Giving.* 12th ed. Chicago, IL: Arthur Andersen, 1995. 43-49.

Ashton, Debra. "Gifts of Securities" in *The Complete Guide to Planned Giving, Everything You Need to Know to Compete Successfully for Major Gifts,* Second Edition. Cambridge, MA: JLA Publications, 1998. 100-109.

Donaldson, David M., Carolyn M. Osteen. "Gifts of Securities" in *The Harvard Manual on Tax Aspects of Charitable Giving,* Seventh Edition. Boston, MA: Harvard University, Publisher, 1992. 401-408.

Hardeman, Mary Todd. *Guide for Donors.* Meadville, PA: Allegheny College, Publisher, 1997. 29 pages.

Chapter 8

Corporate Matching Gifts: From Checking Eligibility to Increasing Their Use

■ By Blossom Gardner
Corporate Matching Gifts Coordinator
Duke University

W hat are matching gifts? That's been the opening question in every book, brochure, and seminar I've ever encountered on the subject, and I've been working with corporate matching gifts (and encountering related books, brochures, and seminars) for 10 years. So here's my definition, though not very original:

A matching gift is an eligible contribution by an eligible corporation on behalf of an eligible employee whose eligible gift to an eligible institution starts the process.

To delve into the history and the *raison d'être* for matching gifts would be preaching to the choir, so I do not intend to spend your time, nor mine, in this pursuit. Rather, we'll concentrate on two aspects of a matching gift program that are not so clear: eligibility (as you can't help noticing the emphasis on the word "eligible" in my definition) and the nuts and bolts of program application. Then we'll explore how to build communication and relationships among all the participants: corporation, institution, employee/donor, and, ultimately, the gift program's real recipient: the student, researcher, or project to which the money goes.

ENSURING ELIGIBILITY

I cannot stress enough how important the word eligible is, both to my definition and to a well-run matching gift program.

Even so, it comes as no surprise that eligibility standards encompass black, white, and shades of gray. Each matching gift corporation sets eligibility according to its own philosophy, the will of its board, and the advice of its financial wizards, and it must do all this while remaining within the legal constants established by the U.S. Internal Revenue Service. Certainly financial constraints shape the way a corporation sets minimum and maximum amounts and ratios as well. Where the going gets rough for both corporation and campus is in two areas: employee and company designations, and gift types.

Surely the most difficult area is employee designation—that is, the program to which employees want to designate their match. If you wish to hold a position as matching gift coordinator, you should first ponder whether you're ready to steel yourself against the arguments that lie ahead. Then you should ask whether your administration will back you when you must say no to, for example, a gift made by a trustee to an ineligible fund, even though such gifts have always been matched in the past.

The most vexing, and prevalent, area of ineligibility is athletic funds. Although there is no legal basis for matching payments made for tuition, pledges, or loans, for instance, donors can conceivably make a case for matching gifts to athletics, especially gifts to scholarship. To begin with, in many cases the employee's donation is as tax-deductible as any other gift. And, too, the money is going for scholarship, albeit athletics-based.

But many companies simply won't permit it. In reply to unhappy donors, the strongest argument you can make is that the matching gift company disallows such gifts under its eligibility requirements. Enough said? Hardly! Yet it must be. To be otherwise would jeopardize the offended company's willingness to match gifts to any program in your institution.

As one who works at a university with a strong athletic program, I can tell you that being the matching gifts coordinator will hardly land you a front-row seat at any sporting event, at least not when you first begin to enforce corporate regulations. But with time, I have found, everyone realizes that a clean program is the way to go. The credibility of the institution as a whole, along with the clear conscience that goes with adhering to the rules, must prevail. The last thing any development effort needs is for the media to raise questions regarding the inappropriate acceptance of gifts to athletics (of all things!). Where should the buck stop? With the verifier of the matching gift forms.

Remember: Matching gifts are a privilege, not a right. A company or foundation can renege any time it so desires. Not only would this hurt financially, but it would also damage your campus's reputation. And there is a monumental, if remote, consideration: the possibility that the offended company could cut off funds to other gifts and grants. That thought should send shudders through the CFO of any nonprofit, especially a research institution that lives by grants.

> *Remember:*
> *Matching gifts are a*
> *privilege, not a right.*
> *A company or*
> *foundation can*
> *renege any time it so*
> *desires.*

Other types of gifts whose eligibility for a match may come into question are building funds, life insurance premiums, gifts-in-kind, deferred gifts, and securities (stocks, bonds, and mutual funds). CASE's *Matching Gift Details* directory is an invaluable source of guidance on this topic. Between *Details* and the information on the company's own matching gift form, you can be reasonably sure of the matchability of a specific gift.

But when in doubt, always, always call the corporate representative. After you do, document the company's name, the date, the eligibility ruling, and the name and title of the person with whom you spoke. Keeping this information on file is your best defense against the "we've always done it this way" syndrome. Also, don't be above calling a second time if necessary, or if so much time has elapsed that a ruling could have changed. Eligibility requirements do shift. Corporations are under no obligation to keep nonprofits apprised of changes, though many times they will. But it is better to err in favor of a clean program than to jeopardize a great relationship with a benefactor.

At Duke, we have a standard procedure when a department and/or donor are adamant that a gift is matchable but the compa-

Creating Your Own Network

When meeting with staff from other nonprofits, I am always surprised at how many ways there are to skin a cat. Forming a consortium of peers who are involved in matching gifts is absolutely the best way to find out what works and what doesn't. It is also a chance to associate with organizations like yours in size, finances, and focus while still being exposed to the methods of disparate groups. Through its Corporate Matching Gifts Symposium, held each spring, CASE offers opportunities to get together with corporations, foundations, and nonprofits from all over to listen and learn.

Perhaps you feel you have the perfect method. Be out with it! Or perhaps you feel you have the unsolvable dilemma. Be out with it! Most of us do not pay our money to sit around and compare successes (well, maybe a little.) We meet as a group primarily to gain knowledge and to ask questions. Never be afraid of either one.

ny has advised the university that it is not. We ask for a letter from the corporation on its letterhead, signed by the officer in charge of the matching program (who may be the matching gift coordinator). The letter states the specifics of the situation: donor, amount of gift, name of area to which the gift is given, and name of area to which the matching gift will be applied. Should this be a case in which the company is willing to make a one-time concession, we ask for a paragraph saying so, and the same thing if repeated exceptions may be made.

By making this a formal, mandatory procedure, you'll help others in your nonprofit come to accept it. Attributing its necessity to campus and corporate auditors, who are naturally concerned about your following the straight and narrow, can curtail much debate among you, the department, and the donor.

I personally have been deceived only one time. The secretary of a donor called and, in an oh-so-timid voice, told me that Mr. So-and-So did have the right to match his gift to Duke. I felt sympathetic toward her being made to tell this untruth so I did not quiz her. I simply asked that the assertion be put in writing and that she sign the letter, using her title. Then, I said, we would put it on file for future reference. I never heard from her, or the truly offending party, the donor.

PROGRAM APPLICATION: PROMOTING AND RECORDING MATCHING GIFTS

The most important, and thus the most difficult, aspect of our work is just getting donors to use their companies' matching gift programs. Of course, in order to use a program, potential donors must first be aware that it exists. Building this awareness is complicated by the fact that corporations do not necessarily advertise that they match gifts. In such cases, word-of-mouth among cronies works great. Let's say you have a loose-knit group of alumni who work for a certain company. They can be a tremendous asset to your matching gift program.

But you cannot depend on just that.

You need to get the word out in a more structured fashion. You need to get employment information on as many donors as possible, wed that information to the matching status of the corporations, and then alert your donors to the greatest deal around: Their company will support their interest in your nonprofit.

All the literature your nonprofit sends out should contain something about matching. For example, if you do a census, you'll naturally ask for employment information, so why not add the question, Does your employer have a matching gift program? Put the notion in your prospects' heads. In mass appeals, a short statement about checking with one's human resources office as to whether a matching program is available has made the difference between receiving $5,000 and $10,000-plus. Never think that just because a program is remarkable, everyone knows about it.

Once you've established that a donor has the ability to match through a company's program, persuading him or her to obtain the matching gift form is the next goal. (For simplicity's sake, here I'll be using donor employment as the typical qualification for gift matching. But don't forget that many corporations also match gifts from spouses, board members, etc.)

Many donors are aware of their companies' benevolence yet do not take the time to obtain a form, complete the donor section, and send it on to the nonprofit. How do you reach these people? Coercion doesn't work—and head development folk will look down on it besides! Persuasion is key. If you can get a donor to match just one gift—the larger, the better—you have him or her hooked on what a terrific perquisite this matching gifts thing really is.

How do you go about this? Think about who is most concerned about the numbers. On campus, it has to be the development officers. These are your pupils! Teach them how much easy money can come from persuading the patrons under their charge to use their companies' matches. Instead of raising $5,000 for the new scholarship, they will have $10,000, or even more in many cases, to show for their efforts. And if there are three such donors who will be making sizable contributions to that scholarship— well, development officers will get the picture.

Work with these staff members. Lend them your support. Never does a day go by that I don't talk with at least one development officer regarding eligibility of a donor, or the parameters of a particular corporate program, or something with regard to matching gifts. I take every opportunity to stress that our working together is good for everybody—and well worth the time.

It's impossible to remember the unique criteria for every matching gift entity.

Once your institution has its donors hooked on matching, you will receive most matching gift forms when you receive the actual gifts. Check carefully to see that the information on the form parallels the gift—for instance, that the donor fills in $100 as the donation when sending a $100 gift. This is usually the work of the gifts clerk, and I will not go into the mechanics of this. But suffice it to say that to protect your credibility, the information should be checked and someone on staff should call the donor to clarify any questionable statements.

It's impossible to remember the unique criteria for every matching gift entity. So your database should include basic information for each matching gift program: address, phone number, contact, and minimum/maximum allowable match. A second record, which can be cued from the first, would include further information, such as whether the company requires a copy of the check, matches gifts to athletics, verifies electronically rather than on paper, and more. These fields should be easy for the input clerk to get to.

Another nettlesome detail involves providing photocopies of checks as required with some matching gift forms. We at Duke do not routinely keep copies of checks below $10,000, so for this reason every return of a form is very time consuming. Getting your act together before you send the form is the ticket! When we receive a gift from a donor who is eligible for a match from a company that requires a check, we make a printout of the donor's employment record with the check copied on the bottom and file the information chronologically. This definitely takes extra effort on our part, but it has paid rewards in the long run.

The other option, calling donors to get them to make a copy of their check, is something we avoid. Our philosophy is to do our best not to bother our donors. They've done their part by giving us money and a matching gift form. We try to take it from there.

Just as someone on staff should head off problems with photocopies of checks, someone should carefully read and complete all information under the recipient organization section so that your friendly matching gift companies needn't spend their valuable time and money calling you or returning forms to you for proper completion. I mention this contritely, for I've been guilty of providing misinformation on occasion. Usually it happens when I'm in a hurry, which never seems to pay.

The actual method you use to handle any of these details is up to your organization. Many times we get mired in the way we've always done it, to the point where we're unable to change. But I think those days are quickly fading. With all the information we now have at our fingertips, we will be expected, and rightly so, to change for efficiency's sake. We'll streamline, but we shouldn't discard old methods until we're sure the new ones really are better.

COMMUNICATION AND CULTIVATING RELATIONSHIPS

Matching gifts make everybody happy, or so they should. Problems arise when the relationships between the parties are not open and above-board. Just as in any relationship, success depends on your understanding others' positions, and their understanding yours.

Some matching gift coordinators tell me they have a hard time getting through to their development officers. So how about contacting their boss? You need somebody with clout to buy into the effectiveness of matching.

If you don't feel comfortable (and perhaps it is not within the pecking order at your institution) speaking directly with, say, the vice president of development, how about a memorandum or report to everyone involved in fund raising? Cite examples from your office and figures from other places that show quite literally

Found Money

I highly recommend keeping a record of all matching gift expectancies, on computer or on paper. Here at Duke we've found it worthwhile to keep paper copies of all matching gift forms, filed according to corporation in alphabetical order by donor. You may think this quite archaic (and that's your right), but there have been many reasons to look back at the actual form.

When a corporate matching coordinator calls me, we're on the same page, quite literally! When we receive the check that corresponds to our form copy and compare it to our copy to make sure everything is correct, we simply recycle the copy. What about the copies that are gathering dust because the match never arrived? We cull them from our files during a slow period in the fiscal year (August is good for us) and call to ask about the status of the match. We also run reports that show unmatched matching expectancies on our system.

Between the paper copies and the reports, we acquire money that would have otherwise fallen through the cracks. There have been years, in fact, when what we collected in this way has far outpaced my annual salary! And these hard copies have made it much easier to go through the list of outdated expectancies. A printout would not show any of the information, including sidebar comments from the input clerks.

the profitability that results from getting the word out about matching.

Sometimes relationship problems arise with the matching gift companies—and once again, this can be because eligibility issues put you in a tight spot between your individual donor and your corporate donor. You must tread carefully without ever allowing the rules to be compromised. Of course, it makes your job harder that the rules change and each corporation seems to have its own criteria.

> *If your organization is doing its job at calling a gift a gift, and a payment a payment, your knowing the difference between the two should be no problem.*

But there are some constants. A major one is that each contribution must be eligible according to the Internal Revenue Service, whose definition of a gift is a voluntary transfer of money or property that is made with no expectation of procuring financial benefit commensurate with the amount of the transfer. Looked at another way, when patrons of fund-raising activities receive consideration in the form of substantial benefits, there is a presumption that any payments they make are not true gifts.

If your organization is doing its job at calling a gift a gift, and a payment a payment, your knowing the difference between the two should be no problem. The issue is whether the matching gift company deems that your donor's gift is eligible. And here lies the potential for relationship problems with the donor. As we've already discussed, the solution is to read the form and, if need be, call the company and ask the folks who make the rules. Simple? You bet. Effective? Tremendously. You build a rapport with an organization that supports your organization. You know the definitive answer, so you can go back to your donor with specifics, including the name of the person at the company who told you emphatically that it does not match gifts to building funds, or to tennis teams, or to a religious center on campus.

Should the area that would have benefited from the denied match, or its esteemed donor, have a problem with the refusal, I suggest a proactive step. If the donor sincerely and adamantly believes that her gift is worthy of matching, then the donor should plead her case to her company. Should there be a reversal, I insist that a letter to that effect be sent to me on company letterhead by the matching gift coordinator. I have seen this work on several occasions: I've gone to bat for the match, been denied, encouraged the employee to try, and succeeded. I've never felt that I failed in this situation but rather that the donor's efforts, combined with mine, made the difference.

Remember, this is a team effort, and we are all on the same team. And this team is working for a cause, which brings me to the real bottom line.

WHO BENEFITS FROM MATCHING GIFTS?

With all this talk of the details of eligibility and what gets matched and what doesn't, can we keep the trees from obscuring the forest?

The fact is, matching gifts are a tribute to our organizations' worth. To be a nonprofit and be eligible for matching gifts, an organization usually serves society in some way or another. Thus many people profit from the nonprofit where you work: the students, the researchers, the faculty, the alumni, and, yes, even paid employees such as yourself. And that's not even counting the link we form with a vast number of service and product industries, from the Federal Express deliverer to the Burger King employee at our student union, and so on.

In our capitalistic society, we are so interlinked that determining specifically who is served is very difficult. But where does the matching money go? To support the main thrust of the organization, in our case education and research. And who profits from this thrust? Everyone—as long as we are fair with each other. To be otherwise would break the chain of benevolence known as matching gifts.

References:

Chambers, Brett. "Public Schools Turn to Fund Raising," *Matching Gift Notes* 12, no. 7 (Fall 1996): 1, 2, 6. ·

CASE. *Matching Gift Details Directory 1997-98*. Washington, DC: CASE 1997. 220 pages.

CASE. *Matching Gift Details for Windows*. Washington, DC: CASE, 1996. Computer software.

CASE. *Matching Gift Leaflet Series 1997-98*. Washington, DC: CASE, 1997.

Dickey, Marilyn. "Free Money: How Charities Can Make the Most of Matching Gifts," *Chronicle of Philanthropy* 9, no. 10 (March 6, 1997): 40-42.

Foundation Center. *Grants for Matching and Challenge Support*. New York, NY: Foundation Center, December 1997. 76 pages.

Garf, Jennifer. "Simplifying the Business of Corporate Philanthropy," *Matching Gift Notes* 12, no. 4 (Spring 1996): 1-2.

Hunt, Penelope, and Jane Prescott-Smith. "Tips for Administering Matching Gifts in a Small Shop," *Matching Gift Notes* 13, no. 2 (Summer/Fall 1997):

Paul, Alison. "Matching Gift Issues for Corporations and Corporate Foundations," *Matching Gift Notes* 12, no. 4 (Spring 1996): 1, 3, 5.

Section III

Stewardship

Chapter 9

Becoming a Good Steward: How to Form Your Rationale and Use the Basic Tools

■ By Debbie Meyers
   Director of Stewardship and Donor Relations and
■ Michael L. House
   Director of Operations, University of Florida Foundation

In a business sense, donor relations means keeping your customers happy. This can require patience, tact, and restraint. It necessitates a true knack for explaining to irate or demanding people everything from gift levels to parking privileges. It may entail organizing a special event, arranging special treatment for donors during football season, and much more.

Donor relations is a catch-all phrase that means strengthening the relationship between your institution and your donors. Stewardship is just one of the many functions of donor relations, and the one this chapter will focus on. As an ethical responsibility, stewardship means making sure your donor knows that you've honored your agreement, and how. It is not the same as cultivation, for you may be obliged to provide stewardship to donors who will never give another gift. In its simplest form, stewardship is the merger of good manners and accountability. It is thanking and reporting, regularly and often.

Although you as the stewardship director are responsible for making sure it gets done, in fact stewardship is a duty that many people share at various levels and in diverse ways. Often, the most appropriate person to handle stewardship is someone outside the development office. But working with administrators, faculty, students, and others to perform stewardship duties is often a challenge. Many do not feel it is their job to thank donors or to keep in touch with them. Likewise, working with development officers to provide stewardship is not always easy. They have many other priorities and administrative duties. They forget things and lose papers. They may be prone to neglecting donors who will not give any more to the institution.

> *Your institution owes a great deal to your donors—past, present, and future.*

Nevertheless, your role is to overcome these problems and work with appropriate staff to get all donors the care and attention they deserve.

Why?

Because even though obvious credit for your institution's success lies with outstanding faculty, researchers, staff, coaches, and students, it has been able to reach its current stature only through the support of generous alumni, loyal friends, grateful patients, and other benefactors.

It owes a great deal to your donors—past, present, and future. Thus you must see to it that it values them in appropriate and meaningful ways.

EXACTLY WHAT IS STEWARDSHIP, AND HOW DOES IT WORK?

Stewardship is the link between the institution and the donor in building trust, credibility, and gratitude through donor recognition and acknowledgment, as well as through fund establishment and enhancement. Or, more simply stated, it is thanking donors and making sure they know how their gifts are being used.

The goals of a good stewardship office are:

1. To make sure it preserves the **institutional memory** about donors and their relationships to the institution. It's crucial to document and maintain central records on all interactions with

donors for anyone who needs that information.

2. To ensure that someone has a **personal relationship** with each donor. Again, the stewardship director doesn't have to do it, but someone must or the donor will have a weak tie to the institution.

3. To function as the **conscience** of the institution. Donors deserve to know that their funds are being used as they requested.

Members of the stewardship staff help identify which donors should receive attention, and how. You can maintain and enhance this connection in a variety of ways—annual endowment reports, stewardship activities, gift club benefits, and other special projects and events. (We'll cover annual endowment reports and stewardship checklists later.)

The mission of any good stewardship office, then, would include:

- Creating and maintaining acknowledgment, recognition, and stewardship programs that are sustainable over time and prove your institution's accountability.
- Developing systems and procedures that encourage collaboration between donor relations staff and development staff.
- Communicating those systems and procedures to development staff and others within your organization.
- Seeking opportunities to offer support and advice on any stewardship and donor relations efforts in any of your organization's sub-units (such as colleges or departments).

STEWARDSHIP TOOLS: SETTING UP SHOP

If you're the institution's stewardship director, it is absolutely crucial that your administration views yours as the main stewardship program. In other words, your supervisors must support the idea that all records and efforts run through your office, not through individual departments, colleges, or units. You cannot monitor what you cannot control. Everyone involved must understand that your office is the clearinghouse for all stewardship activities.

Once you have this mandate, you need to determine what level of stewardship your institution should offer to different types of donors. To do so, ask such questions as:

- Which donors will receive stewardship?

- Will you base what they receive on their gifts' dollar amount? Will that amount reflect cumulative giving or one-time gifts? Will you count deferred gifts at a full dollar amount, or as a percentage?
- Will you treat organizations differently from individuals?
- Will you "layer" stewardship donors by the amount of stewardship they need (high, medium, and low maintenance)? Or will you treat everyone the same?
- Will you treat endowed or unrestricted gifts differently from capital gifts or research funding?

Next, you will need to let development officers know which donors need stewarding and at what level of attention. Even if they choose to do stewardship for donors who fall below your threshold, at a minimum they will need to plan stewardship activities for all donors who meet your institutional requirements. Your computer department can pull these names for you based on whatever criteria you set. For instance, you may request a list of all one-time gifts of $100,000 or more, counting deferred gifts at 20 percent (a $1 million gift annuity would be credited as a $200,000 gift). You may also want to sort these gifts by department or college or unit, depending on where they went and who will steward them. That way it will be easier to distribute lists to the proper steward.

> *Whatever stewardship techniques you choose, remember that at the base of it all is being appreciative.*

If you do have a centralized stewardship program, a helpful tool is a stewardship checklist. Such a list offers development officers a menu of stewardship ideas, organized by types of gifts, to inspire them to make an annual stewardship plan for each of their stewardship donors. (This is a key element of our program at the University of Florida.) The beauty of the checklist system is that it requires development officers to document their stewardship plan for each donor who warrants one. That plan stays in the donor's central file and on the database so that anyone who needs to know that donor's stewardship history will have access to it. It minimizes the negative effects of staff turnover, centralizes the donor's history with the institution, and ensures that the donor has a continual personal relationship with someone.

How development officers implement their plan will depend on your software. Ideally, your fund raisers will have a centralized database that you'll have access to for monitoring purposes.

Specifically, you may wish to order quarterly reports on these donors to see if stewards are actually carrying out their plans, as they should.

Another basic, important tool for a stewardship program is the annual endowment report. This lets donors know the status of their endowed funds. It can be as elaborate or as simple as you wish, but at a minimum, it should report the name of the fund and a meaningful dollar amount (e.g., market value of the endowment). You can base it on a fiscal year or calendar year. Development officers can help you determine which donors should receive this report. (Keep in mind you can send it to more than one donor and to the survivors or estate representative of a deceased donor.) Whatever information you choose to include, be sure donors at all levels of financial acumen understand what the figures mean.

Along with the report, you may wish to enclose a letter that gives more detail about how the funds are being expended. For example, the endowment report may tell John Anderson that the John Anderson Scholarship Fund had a fiscal year-end market value of $110,342. But the accompanying letter can tell him that five students received $2,000 scholarships as a result of his gen- erosity. The letter could elaborate on who the students are as well as where they're from, their year of study, and their major and career goals. Such a letter adds a human touch to the report's financial information. (It's nice to have both!)

Want more stewardship ideas? Special events, gift clubs, publications, and functions are as diverse as the institutions that sponsor them. Many have scholarship luncheons at which donors and their scholarship recipients or endowed professors meet face to face. Some list their donors in brochures or on Internet sites. Still others send their donors videos of buildings or of students and professors thanking them for their gifts. The sky is truly the limit when it comes to creativity.

If you have e-mail access, a great idea resource is a listserv. For example, Stewardshiplist, hosted by Southern Methodist University, is for those who are interested in stewardship and donor relations at nonprofits. To subscribe, send an e-mail message to *majordomo@mail.smu.edu*. Leave the subject header blank, and in the message text, type *subscribe stewardshiplist*.

Whatever stewardship techniques you choose, remember that

Why Stewardship Matters: A Case Study

Your stewardship efforts, or lack of them, may mirror how strategically your institution handles your best supporters. What would happen in the long term to an organization with no stewardship program? Imagine the following scenario.

Your university president and a development officer (DO) visit a donor to present him with a $1 million proposal. The donor reads the proposal, throws it down on the table, and says indignantly, "How dare you ask me for more money? You haven't contacted me since I contributed 10 years ago! I hear from you only when you want something."

Stunned, the president and DO walk out of his office and fly back home. Very uncomfortable trip for the DO! "How could this happen?" the president demands. "Don't we have programs in place to thank our donors? Why has no one been to see this man in over 10 years?"

The DO, who's has been at the university for three years, knows for a fact that she did visit the donor once, and a professor from her college has written him several times. She vaguely recalls that the previous DO had interactions with this donor as well. But how can she defend herself against the president's accusations?

This story could have two endings.

- **The sad ending:** The DO realizes that she never filed a contact report on her visit, so she cannot prove to the president that she was ever there. The university has no donor database, so she cannot find out who has met with this donor in the past. The professor is on sabbatical and out of the country, so she cannot reach him. The previous DO took all his files with him when he left, so there is no record of his interaction with this donor. All she can find is a copy of a letter she sent the donor a year ago inviting him to an event on campus. That's it! She has no way of proving that she or anyone else had any contact with this donor.

- **The happy ending:** The DO returns to her office and goes directly to the stewardship director, who provides her with copies of annual endowment reports that were mailed to the donor each year since he made his gift. The stewardship director also provides the DO with copies of her stewardship checklist activities for the past three years. These copies show the DO's annual stewardship plan for that donor, including details of visits and contact reports. From the database, the stewardship director also pulls contact reports from the previous DO. Through all this documentation, the DO and stewardship director have a mountain of evidence that the university had indeed been in touch with the donor.

You hope that no DO at your institution will ever have to mount such a defense. But even if no one does, this story still teaches three important lessons about stewardship.

1. To be effective, stewardship needs to be a centralized, programmed, documented list of activities. An organization with a strong stewardship program will not suffer when staff turns over.

2. Your staff members need to know what programs are in place to help them do their jobs. Had the president and DO known about all the routine institutional stewardship activities, they could have responded better on the spot to the donor's complaint.

3. When it comes to defining an adequate level of stewardship, what you perceive and what the donor perceives may be entirely different. In this case, the donor did receive frequent visits and reports, but in his mind, these were not enough. And if the DO can't remember what she's done, then it definitely wasn't enough!

at the base of it all is being appreciative. It doesn't matter how old the gift is, or that you weren't even born when the gift was donated. It doesn't matter if the donor will never give another cent. It doesn't matter that you weren't the development officer when that donor gave.

What matters is that someone from your institution tells the donor, "Thank you. We care about you. Here's how your generosity has changed many lives."

References:

Clotfelter, Susan. "Working for the Weekend: A Carefully Planned Major Donor Weekend Program Can Bring More Than Money to Your Campus," CURRENTS 16, no. 10 (November/December 1990): 44-50.

CASE. *Donor Bill of Rights.* CASE, 1994.

Dessoff, Alan L. "Put It in Writing: Don't Let Donor Thanks Fall by the Wayside. Create a Written Recognition Policy to Make Thank-Yous a Part of Your Development Office Routine," CURRENTS 23, no. 2 (February 1997): 30-34.

Dunlop, David R. "The Ultimate Gift: The Biggest Gifts of All Take a Special Kind of Fund Raising, CURRENTS 13, no. 5 (May 1987): 8-13.

Hampton, Cathy. "First-Class Stewardship: Cultivate Not Only Great Prospects But Also Great Donors—And Make Room at the Top for More," CURRENTS 15, no. 5 (May 1989): 58-61.

Hartsook, Robert F. "But Have You Really Said Thank You?: Good Stewardship Is Not Just Sending a Receipt for a Gift. Think of Unique Ways to Say Thank You to Donors," *Fund Raising Management* 26, no. 1 (March 1995): 42-

Henderson, Nancy. "Friend Raising in the College Years: Cultivation Advice for Independent Schools," CURRENTS 23, no. 1 (January 1997): 45.

Henderson, Nancy. "With a Little Help from Your Friends: Can You Get Gifts From Neighbors, Vendors, and Community Groups? Yes—If You're Organized and Willing to Meet Them Halfway," CURRENTS 21, no. 1 (January 1995): 50-55.

House, Michael L. "Structured Stewardship: How One Campus Plugged In a System to Thank, Inform, and Remember Its Top Donors—All Year, Every Year," CURRENTS 22, no. 4 (April 1996): 40-42, 44.

Kirkman, Kay. "Thanks Again—And Again: Seven Simple Steps to a Successful Donor Recognition Program," CURRENTS 21, no. 8 (September 1995): 38-40.

Muir, Roy and Jerry May. *Developing an Effective Major Gift Program: From Managing Staff to Soliciting Gifts.* Edited by Roy Muir and Jerry May. Washington, DC: CASE, 1993. 134 pages.

Ostrower, Francie. *Why the Wealthy Give: The Culture of Elite Philanthropy*. Princeton, NJ: Princeton University Press, 1996.

Panas, Jerold. Mega Gifts: *Who Gives Them, Who Gets Them*. Chicago, IL: Pluribus Press, 1986. 224 pages.

Pugel, Mary E. "Keep Those Cards and Letters Going: Give Donors What They Expect and Deserve—Old-Fashioned Thank-You Letters," CURRENTS 13, no. 3 (March 1987): 38-40.

Reilly, Thomas J. "Million-Dollar Motivations: A Researcher Asks 30 Top Givers What Prompted Their Generosity," CURRENTS 21, no. 1 (January 1995): 10-15.

Ryan, Ellen. "Courtship Rituals: Chats, Visits, Long Walks Around Campus...How Two Institutions Wooed and Won Top Donors," CURRENTS 22, no. 10 (November/December 1996): 18-20, 22.

Ryan, Ellen. "Many Means of Thanks: Donor Recognition Doesn't Have to Be Expensive—But It Must Be Personal and Sincere. Five Examples Tell the Tale," CURRENTS 21, no. 8 (September 1995): 41-42.

Ryan, J. Patrick. "Thanks a Million: You Need Strong Recognition Programs to Foster Healthy Donor Relations," CURRENTS 20, no. 3 (March 1994): 64.

Shubeck, Theresa. "For Donors Who Have Everything: Major Givers Hardly Need Another Bronze Plaque. Here's How to Say Thank You With Sincerity and Creativity," CURRENTS 16, no. 10 (November/December 1990): 52-57.

Taylor, Karla. *Donor Relations The Essential Guide To Stewardship Policies, Procedures, and Protocol*. Washington, DC.: CASE Books, 1999. 97 pages.

Thomas, Susan Decker. "Do You Hear What I Hear? Prospects Will Indicate When They're Open to the Idea of Planned Gifts. Here's How to Recognize Their Cues and Respond Appropriately," CURRENTS 24, no. 3 (March 1998): 36-40.

Chapter 10

The Art of Saying Thank You

■ By Kelley Rickard
Assistant Director of Development
Georgetown Preparatory School

Thanking donors is not an option. It's an obligation.

These are strong words, but very true. If your organization doesn't show donors that you appreciate their making the time and effort to give, their future gifts will surely go elsewhere. As an advancement officer, you are throwing money out the window.

I have never met a donor who said, "Enough already. Please don't send me another thank-you letter, phone call, or invitation to a special dinner. You are doing too much for me already." Donors like to be thanked. They want to feel appreciated and know they're helping to facilitate a good cause. So the question is not, "Should you say thank you?" The question is, "How and how much?"

SAYING THANKS IN WRITING

According to the IRS, it is the nonprofit's responsibility to provide a receipt for all gifts greater than or equal to $250. To comply with the law, you must send a receipt for these gifts. So it's logical to send a thank-you letter along with the receipt. [For more on official wording that the IRS finds acceptable, see Chapter 6.]

Too many institutions fail to send an acknowledgment if a gift is worth less than $250. This is wrong. Sending $50 or $100 is a stretch for some donors, whether because they're young, on a fixed income, or for other reasons. It is vital that these individuals know you appreciate their gift as much as a multi-millionaire's $50,000 check. If you overlook the small donor, you're also overlooking future gifts.

> **You must send all donors a thank-you letter, ideally within 24 hours of receipt of the gift.**

For example, let's say Mr. Smith graduated from your institution in 1946. For 10 years, without fail, he sent in a $100 donation on November 19. Due to the small size of his contributions, your office never sent a thank-you letter nor researched his name for wealth potential.

Then one year, after the gifts had stopped, an observant researcher happened to spot his name in an obituary. The researcher dug a little deeper and learned that not only was Mr. Smith worth several million dollars, but he left the majority of his estate to several educational institutions. Not yours, though. November 19 was the anniversary of his marriage to his wife, also a graduate of your campus, who passed away 10 years ago. In fact, they met and fell in love on your campus. If Mr. Smith had received a kind thank-you from someone at your institution at some point over the past 10 years, he no doubt would have left a portion of his estate to the campus.

This fictitious tale is a reality for many nonprofits, even if they don't know it. In this technological age, there is no excuse for failing to cultivate future gifts by sending every donor a thank-you. All institutions have the capability to purchase a database that allows it to personalize a form thank-you letter for all donors. Even a basic word-processing program is capable of storing a small database of donor names and addresses.

So the lesson is clear: You must send all donors a thank-you letter, ideally within 24 hours of receipt of the gift. The next question is, who should sign it?

The answer varies from institution to institution, but one aspect stays the same. No matter if the person issuing the thank-you is the president, dean of students, board member, department head, director of development, or another institutional leader, he or she should have a meaningful relationship to the donor.

At our school, Georgetown Prep, the president signs every thank-you letter personally. What's more, he writes a note on each. True, our institution is small; we process only about 2,000 annual fund gifts each year. But we can't help noticing the overwhelmingly positive response from both our donors and our president. He understands the need for personalization and is willing to sacrifice time and hand cramps (especially in December) to give donors what they deserve: personal recognition.

At larger institutions, obviously, more than one person would need to be responsible for personalizing letters. Paying attention to such details is still worth it, however. Doing so makes your institution stand out from others that are unwilling to be generous with their efforts for donors.

In addition to sending a formal letter from an institutional leader, many campuses have scholarship recipients write thank-yous. This simple touch means so much to donors, and it's also a good learning opportunity for students. They acquire a real feel for how their education is being funded as they learn about the concept of philanthropy. It is a first step toward molding future donors.

SAYING THANKS BY PHONE AND IN PERSON

In this age of telephone solicitors, wouldn't it be nice to hear a friendly voice thanking you for a gift instead of asking for money? That's why many institutions have thank-a-thons. A group of students calls annual donors to express appreciation for gifts that they've already made. No ask is involved.

If a thank-a-thon is inconceivable, recruit a handful of trusted faculty, board members, development officers, etc., to call major donors. Many institutional leaders are already familiar with major donors from the community or the campus. Donors appreciate both the time these leaders take as well as the evidence that their gifts didn't get lost in the shuffle.

At Georgetown Prep, our president personally calls major

donors to thank them. He times his phone calls to take place soon after his written thanks arrives in the mail. The phone call and letter are opportunities for a relationship to bloom.

One other time to offer personal thanks is when donors visit campus. They often attend sporting events, art exhibits, and theatrical performances, among many other activities. Assign development officers or others to attend various events, seek donors out, and simply talk to them. The goal is to speak to as many donors as possible in a friendly, non-threatening manner. What a wonderful feeling for them to be known and welcomed on their own campus.

When you do meet donors informally, remember why the old adage "a smile is worth a thousand words" appears in so many employee manuals in the hospitality field: because it works! A simple smile is a nonverbal thank-you: a way to show sincere appreciation.

Also keep in mind how revealing body language can be. If you constantly look over a donor's shoulder while in conversation, he or she will quickly assume you'd rather be somewhere else. Everything you do must signal the fact that you're responsive to donors' needs and wants. By paying attention to them, you prove that you hold them in high regard.

RESPONDING TO GIFTS WITH A GIFT

When you're thinking beyond words to tokens of appreciation, keep in mind the need to say thank-you appropriately. On a grand scale, let's say a donor contributes a large gift to name a new building. Does he want nothing more than a small, private thank-you luncheon with the president? Arrange that function and that alone. Would he feel slighted with anything less than a large public dedication ceremony? When you get the gut feeling that a donor is going to need additional attention, give it.

There's a multitude of other tangible ways to say thank you. Use your imagination; many options cost little or nothing. For example, invite donors to sit in on a class or take a tour of the campus. Send them free tickets to plays, concerts, or sporting events, depending on what appeals to them most. Or invite them to volunteer or advise. There is no greater way to show someone you

A simple smile is a nonverbal thank-you: a way to show sincere appreciation.

appreciate their time, energy, and intellect than to ask their opinion.

A popular way to show thanks is to publish a list of donors in an annual report for the entire community to see. Almost every institution does this because not only is it a simple form of appreciation, but people also enjoy reading their own names. Even so, always be mindful of donors who wish to remain anonymous.

Two words of caution about thank-you tokens. Keep in mind the IRS restrictions on *quid pro quo* gifts. You must be aware that despite your good intentions, some thank-yous may well reduce a donation's tax-deductibility. For more on this topic, again see Chapter 6.

The IRS aside, don't feel you have to give every donor something. Most would rather know their entire gift is going to the specified cause. So, unlike notes and in-person gestures, thank-you tokens should be used sparingly. Not only will donors appreciate your common-sense approach, but when you do lavish them with something special, they will appreciate it more.

The Rules in Review

- Personalize every thank-you letter. If at all possible, have the person who signs the letter add a personal note.
- Send written thank-yous within 24 hours. In the case of major gifts, have an appropriate person follow up with a phone call.
- Make sure that more than one person acknowledges major gifts, and do it in a variety of forms. For example, after the department head mails out a thank-you, the director of development could place a personal call, and then the president could issue an invitation to an annual dinner.
- Whenever possible, actually speak to donors. Ask students to participate in a thank-a-thon. Recruit the board of trustees' development subcommittee to call major donors. Remember that actions speak louder than words. Smile, shake hands, and go out of your way to be sociable with donors.
- Encourage supporters to contribute in a wide variety of ways, not just by giving money. Show that you appreciate them for their expertise and advice.
- Use thank-you gifts and tokens sparingly. Not only are there IRS ramifications, but donors would also rather see their money used for a worthy cause.
- Publish a list of donors at least once a year. Make sure they know you're going to do this so they can inform you if they wish to remain anonymous.
- Don't forget that activities are an additional way to say thank-you. Invite donors to lectures, luncheons, dinners, and VIP seating for theatrical performances or athletic games.
- Last but not least: Be sincere.

THE SECRETS TO SUCCESS: CREATIVITY AND CONTACT

Remember, your problem can never be that you send too many thank-yous. Rather, you may be sending too many of the same type. So encourage your institution to expand the way it says thanks. Involve many levels of staff, volunteers, and students.

Remember, too, that personal contact is always best. Whenever possible, speak to donors and find out why they make gifts. Their words can help you, as a development officer, focus on the true meaning of your work. They let you look beyond the long hours, endless research, and pounds of cheese and cocktail franks. You need to continually be reminded of the devotion so many donors feel toward your institution and their desire to support it in every way they can.

Chapter 11

Ten Ways to Make Thank-You Letters More Personal

■ By Judson Matthews
Alumni Development Consultant
Systems and Computer Technology Corporation
(Formerly Director of Advancement Services at The Citadel)

1. START BY BEING ALERT TO OPPORTUNITIES TO PERSONALIZE.

It's true that your ability to customize your thank-yous is determined by your staff, your computer system, and your administration's willingness to be involved. Even so, I believe poor communication is the most common reason why development officers miss the chance to personalize. How many times have you sent a thank-you and then found out that the donor is involved with your organization in other ways you should have noted?

When we received a gift at The Citadel, where I used to work, we headed off this problem by examining our databases to determine, for example, whether the donor was a board or advisory member, member of the legislature, major donor, potential major donor, or active alumnus. If we found an existing relationship, we in advancement services asked the signer to add a pertinent handwritten comment at the bottom of the letter and, depending on how familiar the signer was with the donor, cross through the typed, formal name in the salutation and write in the donor's informal name.

2. PAY ATTENTION TO THE PURPOSE OF THE GIFT.

The donor's motivation often signals an instant opportunity to personalize. True, an unrestricted gift doesn't offer you many clues. But for most restricted gifts you'll be able to come up with other individuals on campus who are directly or indirectly associated with the donation's purpose.

For example, The Citadel's civil engineering department actively contacted local businesses to raise money for an annual competition. When a business supported the competition, our office, the head of civil engineering, and several students all wrote to say thank you. By having so many people thank the donor, we sent a unified message about how much we appreciated the gift.

When we conducted solicitations for specific programs, such as a parent's appeal or president's appeal, we were equally careful to monitor both what the thank-you letters said and who signed them. If donors were parents, we incorporated their children's names and class year. For gifts to our president's appeal, our president hand-signed all acknowledgments.

3. PAY ATTENTION TO THE AMOUNT OF THE GIFT.

Everyone agrees that all gifts are important. However, because large gifts have the greatest impact and campus leaders have limited time, you'll probably use a dollar scale to determine which official should sign which thank-yous.

At The Citadel, every donor got a signed acknowledgment (which also served as the tax receipt) from the vice president for advancement and, if relevant, a dean or department chair. We averaged around 3,000 gifts a year, so hand-signing was fairly manageable. As the gift volume increases, the staff will have to assess whether to use signature fonts instead of original signatures.

But donors who gave $1,000 or more, or were standouts for other reasons (such as being board members or another type of VIP), got an additional thank-you from the president. The advancement office drafted these extra letters for the president to sign.

4. CHOOSE THE RIGHT PERSON TO DO THE ACKNOWLEDGING.

Often you hear people say you can never thank a donor enough. We like to think you can never have enough of the right people thanking your donor. As I mentioned above, if an opportunity existed, we would get a dean, a department head, or other appropriate college officials involved in sending their own personal acknowledgment. Our advancement office didn't mind providing drafts or examples of letters for their use.

5. MAKE YOUR THANK-YOUS MATCH THE TIME OF YEAR.

Holidays and the changing seasons present unique opportunities to thank donors creatively. For example, one coworker's previous employer used to send acknowledgments on Christmas cards instead of traditional letterhead and got numerous positive comments in response.

6. USE YOUR COMPUTER SYSTEM TO AUTOMATE AS MUCH AS POSSIBLE WITHOUT LOSING SIGHT OF THE PERSONAL TOUCH.

As we all know, assigning unique codes to each type of constituent allows you to segment acknowledgements easily. Even so, this requires detailed identification of every phase of the acknowledgment process. You need to verify that the targeted group is being segmented, the output file is in the correct format, and the word-processing application is capable of easily converting or merging the data file into a letter.

For ease of formatting, The Citadel's personalized acknowledgements typically contained two paragraphs. The first thanked the donor for the gift and described the gift amount and purpose. The second was more personal; it detailed how the gift would benefit our organization. Also, if applicable, we would say in the second paragraph whom the gift would benefit.

By the way, another way we gave a personalized touch was by rewriting our acknowledgements every quarter. This minimized the possibility that a donor might receive the same letter within a year.

7. LET AS MANY PEOPLE AS POSSIBLE CHECK YOUR WORK.

We had six sets of eyes review each acknowledgement that left our office: those of our advancement vice president; our directors of major gifts, corporate and foundations, donor relations, advancement services; and our gift and acknowledgment specialist.

8. STRIVE FOR TOTAL ACCURACY.

Wrong information makes donors think your organization doesn't care about them or their gifts. As you increase the level of automated personalization, you increase your need to pay close attention to detail.

9. CUT DOWN YOUR TURN-AROUND TIME.

By producing and mailing thank-yous quickly, you give donors the message that you care very much about their gifts. We tried to create and mail thank-yous within three working days, which we managed with the help of automation and communication.

10. STAY FLEXIBLE.

Even if you've developed a thank-you process that works for 99 percent of your donors, you'll still have that 1 percent who deserve a gesture above and beyond the usual approach. Often those special donors can make or break your reputation.

References

Kirkman, Kay. "Thanks Again and Again," CURRENTS. (September 1995): 38-40.

Hampton, Cathy. "First-Class Stewardship," CURRENTS (May 1989): 59-61.

Broce, Thomas E. *Fund Raising*. Norman, OK: University of Oklahoma Press, 1979.

DeLong, Mary Lou. Presentation on "Gift Stewardship and Donor Recognition," CASE Summer Institute in Educational Fund Raising, July 1993.

Advancement Services

Section IV

Technology

Chapter 12

Evaluating and Selecting Primary Development Software

■ By Charlie Hunsaker
  President, R I Arlington
■ Jim Williamson
  President, Williamson Consulting, Inc.

H aving been involved in a hundred or more successful software selection projects, we believe we have some useful experience to share. (We've learned a thing or two from the less successful projects, too). The challenge of evaluating and selecting your development office's primary software system has a number of key aspects to it. We'd like to cover this challenge in three parts: checking your sanity in even considering such a project, following a proven process once you've decided to go ahead, and highlighting what we've found to be the key factors in successful selection projects.

But even before we get into the process, let's ask an important question in the decision to acquire a new system.

ARE YOU CRAZY?

Identifying and then implementing an information system will take perhaps two or three years. The process will be expensive, difficult, and, at times, frustrating. You most assuredly will ask yourself numerous times why on earth you got involved in this project.

Even so, the potential benefits to your organization could be significant, and who knows? The project might even end up being fun!

Before you begin, however, you need to ask yourself a number of questions.

- **Should you really acquire a new system?** What's wrong with your old one? Can you articulate the enhancements that could benefit your organization? Is there a problem you're trying to solve?

> *A basic rule of systems implementation is that the process should be in sync with what's going on in the fund-raising program.*

In our experience, a high percentage of the problems that staff members perceive as system deficiencies are related to—if not caused by—organizational and human resources issues. Often, these supposedly poor systems lack enough trained users, good documentation, effective management, or all three. It certainly would be easier to hire the right staff, develop the documentation, and train the users than to acquire a new system. Are you sure those steps wouldn't go a long way toward solving your problems?

- **Is now really the time?** OK, so you're sure you need a new system. But should you do it now? A basic rule of systems implementation is that the process should be in sync with what's going on in the fund-raising program. It always takes longer to convert to a new system than you anticipate. If you have a major campaign in the near future, you might want to think about waiting until the campaign is over before moving forward with a system. (We realize that the next campaign may be the reason you are looking at a new system.)

When you're projecting an implementation schedule, don't listen to the vendors. They'll often say it will take six months or so. In reality, experience shows that at most organizations, going from team formation to full implementation actually takes 18 to 24 months. A complex university with decentralized fund raising but centralized services could easily take 36 months or longer.

- **Where is your organization heading?** The purpose of a development information system is not to manage information. It's to implement the fund-raising business plan. Managing information—address changes, gift processing, acknowledgments—is easy. Implementing a system to support a comprehensive fund-raising program can be very complex.

Does your office have a five-year business plan? If not, stop and develop one before you proceed any further. A realistic plan will better prepare you to select a system appropriate for your needs. Far too many organizations buy systems that have complex capabilities no one will ever use. A plan will help you determine which choice to make: an information system capable of supporting a complex campaign with a regional component, decentralized constituent-based fund raising, and significant corporation and foundation fund raising—or one that only needs to handle alumni relations and an annual fund.

- **What are the givens?** Is there already a winner? Beware of a rigged process in which you expend lots of resources only to find out that there was a preferred vendor all along. Don't waste staff's time if senior management has already chosen a vendor system. But don't expect the staff's buy-in if the decision is made without them.

It's also important to identify, at the beginning, the technical environment within which your new system must work. Does your campus have an information technology plan? Is there a clearly articulated overarching technology? Is there a "preferred" (or dictated) technology standard for your campus? If such a plan exists, stick within it. Don't be the only office on campus with a particular database back-end. Don't buy a system that requires a particular kind of server (e.g. Unix, NT) unless such servers already exist on your campus.

Is there any serious discussion about developing your own fund-raising system rather than purchasing a commercial product? If so, update your resume and get off the team. While the topic of "build vs. buy" was worth discussing 10 years ago, today you should see it as a red flag. That's because it will cost more to develop (and document and support) a custom-designed system than to buy one. Experience shows that few in-house projects succeed. While it's true that custom-designed systems generally meet current organizational needs, rarely can they keep pace with changes in technology as well as advances in development as well as vendor-supported systems.

Among other classic discussions is whether a campus should buy a single integrated system or allow each administrative office to purchase the "best of breed." From a development office viewpoint, you should lobby for a best-of-breed approach to give yourself maximum flexibility. While some excellent single-vendor solutions are available (though few are truly integrated), chances are that if the campus is looking for a single-vendor solution, your student records or finance office will drive the decision. You in development will have to take whatever fund-raising package comes as part of the package. Lobbying for best-of-breed allows you to look at both the stand-alone and integrated choices and see what fits your needs.

OK, you've decided that regardless of this sanity check, you are going to proceed with the project. What's next?

> *Among other classic discussions is whether a campus should buy a single integrated system or allow each administrative office to purchase the "best of breed."*

THE SELECTION PROCESS

How you actually handle your system selection depends on your organization's size and complexity. However, it's important that whatever process you use, it must be documented and supported by the senior administration. Seriously flawed implementations are almost always traceable to a flawed process or the lack of true top-level support for the process (or the team!)

Before You Start

The following section details all the project plan ingredients that would work for most institutions. If, however, your organization is simply too small for such a process, remember these three basic rules that apply to any organization:

1. Form a committee. Don't try to do it alone!
2. Call the vendors last. Don't start by collecting information from vendors.
3. Never allow the vendors on campus until you've docu-

mented your needs, checked several references, and determined that the vendor might be an appropriate solution. (Far too many people purchase a system because of their relationship with the salesperson rather than the functionality of the software).

What are the Steps?

Generally, selection is a two-phase process. Phase I is defining your needs and communicating them to potential vendors. Phase II is evaluating the vendor's bids and systems to see how well they meet your needs. This is all you need to do to make a decision. In the following sections, we'll outline the primary activities and steps that we've found useful in the process.

Phase I: Defining Your Needs and Communicating with Vendors

PLANNING AND ADMINISTRATION

These flow through both phases of the project. You must establish the framework of people, reporting relationships, and responsibilities. You'll monitor project efforts and results to periodically inform the systems committee (and management) of the project status. The project leader must obtain timely decisions and approvals to keep the project on schedule. Then the final results must be presented to management at the end of the project. In sum, the steps in this activity are:

1. Establish a systems committee.
2. Establish the project team.
3. Organize the project with a work plan and reporting assignments.
4. Monitor status on an ongoing basis.
5. Make a final report/presentation to management.

Once you've gotten yourself organized, you're ready to move into the meat of Phase I, the needs definition.

DOCUMENTING AND UNDERSTANDING BUSINESS OBJECTIVES

As no project should be done in a vacuum, this is the first activity you should perform in the needs definition. Obtain a clear understanding of the business environment and plans for which systems are being considered. Also, determine the benefits that management wishes to achieve through automation. Steps in this activity include:

1. Evaluate the present scope of operations.
2. Review existing plans for campaigns, technology changes, organization, etc.
3. Document management's objectives for undertaking the selection project.
4. Identify criteria for evaluating system selection/installation priorities.

DETERMINING INFORMATION AND PROCESSING NEEDS

Through interviews with users, find out what automation support they need to perform, monitor, and control their operations. The systems committee must consider information and processing needs at all levels, from day-to-day operations through management reporting to strategic planning. Steps in this activity include:

1. Prepare for interviews.
2. Conduct interviews.
3. Document findings.
4. Summarize functional requirements and information needs.

DOCUMENTING THE PRESENT STATUS

In certain situations it's appropriate to take this step. It means to identify and quantify the current environment, including hardware, software, people, practices, and their associated costs. This is the benchmark for evaluating a new system. Often, this can provide the baseline, the proverbial stake in the ground from which to measure future successes. It can also provide vital existing cost benchmarks that can feed into a cost/benefit analysis (if the board makes you do one).

Our experience is that once you start documenting business processes, you may realize that some things are broken and need to be fixed (the dreaded "re-engineering"). This is frequently true about gift-processing procedures, or acknowledgment or stewardship procedures. If you uncover significant problems, our strong recommendation is that you fix them before moving forward. If you have information stored in a shoebox, you will have difficulty implementing a new system—it's very difficult to computerize a shoebox.

But in some institutions and situations, you can bypass the entire step of documenting the as-is status. For example, in the late 1990s when institutions saw that their old systems were not Year 2000 compliant, the solution could be summed up as "we've got to replace the system!" However, if you need to identify your current situation, you should do the following:

1. Document existing information systems.
2. Document systems skill levels.
3. Prepare technical analysis.
4. Document current costs.

Through interviews with users, find out what automation support they need to perform, monitor, and control their operations.

IDENTIFYING HARDWARE AND SOFTWARE STRATEGIES

You'll spell out these strategies along with the advantages and constraints that would recommend for or against each. Document the recommended directions. The classic advice is to pick the software and then the hardware to run it on. If you're following that sound approach, you'll take the following steps:

1. Document known systems alternatives.
2. Explore/evaluate software approach alternatives.
3. Explore/evaluate hardware alternatives.
4. Summarize recommended strategies.

If you have a significant fixed investment in hardware, networks, or operating systems (along with the associated expertise in them)—or, as indicated earlier, if an articulated IT strategy exists for administrative systems—you may forgo all of this detailed analysis. Merely say, "The new development software must be consistent with our institution's IT directions." Luckily, as long as you stick with one of the industry-standard approaches, you should be able to find excellent software that fits into the overall scheme.

DOCUMENTING SUPPORTING SYSTEMS PROJECTS

This is a useful activity that some institutions pursue as part of a selection project. In addition to adding a new software package, you may need to make other changes. Remember the questions we told you to ask before starting the project? Are there problems with data quality, policies and procedures, organization, staffing, or inadequate training? If so, identify and describe all projects to be considered to help assure the success of the system selection and implementation efforts. Summarize them in an overall plan

with the following steps:
1. Develop an overall systems strategy.
2. Prepare project descriptions.
3. Summarize costs and benefits.
4. Draft plan.

Documenting the requirements definition/RFP

With this step, you pull together one of the formal work products that comes out of the needs definition phase. Format all requirements (functional, technical, security, performance, support, cost, contractual, and others) into a request for proposals (RFP) for vendor response. Structure the RFP to facilitate evaluation of vendor responses. So, here's the sequence:
1. Update/confirm functional requirements.
2. Prepare the RFP.
3. Solicit vendors.

You can put the RFP in a multitude of formats. Your purchasing department may dictate some of the constraints. CASE, Educause, and other organizations can provide you examples. But don't kill yourself developing the RFP; the vendors will say they can do everything anyway.

One approach we've used with some clients is to focus on documenting uniqueness. Don't spend energy specifying the need for multiple salutations or seasonal address management. If your vendor candidates can't do those things, you've selected the wrong list of vendors. Focus on your unique requirements (such as the bizarre golf tournament/auction you run every year, the fact that you credit 50 percent of a campaign gift to the alumnus's class totals but not to the alumnus's annual fund gift total, etc.). Then just presume the vendors can handle the rest. This is where a consultant may be of help to determine what's standard vs. what is unique to you.

Developing demonstration scenarios and scripts

This step runs concurrently with developing the RFP. Given that vendors often respond to most aspects of an RFP in the affirmative, it's important to lay out a demonstration process that will let users confirm that a certain vendor's system can meet their needs. This set of activities will structure the demonstration process for the most effective evaluation:

1. Outline the framework of scenarios by functional area.
2. Translate requirements into scenarios with detailed scripts.
3. Identify selected data for the scripts.
4. Publish the scenarios/scripts.

Such a scenario will allow you to control the demonstration and minimize the hype. You might find it helpful to block out a short time, say 30 minutes, for the vendor to pitch her firm and why it's the best option for you. But you should dedicate the rest of the time to proving their ability to meet your needs.

Phase I concludes as you send out the RFP to vendors. While you're waiting for their responses, you can complete the demonstration scenarios. You'll send these only to the vendor finalists whom you'll invite to demonstrate their systems at your site.

Phase II: Evaluation and Contracting

EVALUATING VENDORS AND SYSTEMS

In this first step of Phase II, you must confirm the ability of both vendor and system to meet your needs. You should verify this in as many ways as possible: proposal review, demos, site visits, and calls to other users. If you don't uncover one vendor who's able to meet all requirements, evaluate other alternatives to meet secondary requirements. Often, the selection committee performs these steps in varying order and as part of an iterative process:

1. Review proposals.
2. Identify vendors for further evaluation.
3. Finalize functional evaluation.
4. Contact references (three to five per vendor system).
5. Evaluate technical considerations.
6. Conduct demonstrations and site visits.
7. Evaluate add-on and stand-alone packages.

SELECTING AND CONTRACTING WITH A VENDOR

You've finally completed the evaluation steps and chosen the vendor/system(s) that best meet your needs. Now work with the vendor(s) to prepare and execute a contract for hardware, software, and all aspects of implementation. Here are your steps:

1. Identify your vendor of choice—preliminarily.
2. Prepare for contract negotiation.
3. Negotiate contract.
4. Contract with the vendor(s) of choice.

Recognize that once you've made the selection, the easy part is over. To prepare for the hard part, the last activity in system selection is this plan. Define and quantify the work you need to implement the system. Assign responsibilities among client, vendor, and consultant/third party personnel. Then schedule the work, balancing effort and resources available, and complete the following steps:

1. Prepare the overall implementation plan.
2. Develop a detailed work plan for priority systems and applications.

CRITICAL SUCCESS FACTORS

From our experience, we know that it's important to consider a phased approach to the selection project and to use a proven process. You may not follow all of the steps above, but ignoring one should be a conscious decision rather than a careless oversight. Murphy's law has a direct impact on any forgotten steps!

Beyond this process, we'd like to highlight several critical success factors. We touched on a number of questions to be considered at the beginning of the chapter. In addition, you will want to give special consideration to the following areas.

Organizing the project

The section above talks about organizing the work. But you also need to think about organizing the people. The most successful projects—both selection and implementation—have a high-level management steering committee overseeing the whole thing.

This steering committee makes sure the project stays on track, helps balance project time demands against day-to-day operational priorities, and receives the actual recommendation about which system to purchase. People from both development and MIS, with titles like VP and senior director, will be on the steering committee. The project leader may also be on the committee and keeps members apprised of progress, accomplishments—and, yes, any problems as well as recommended solutions.

Often, as part of the steering committee, many organizations identify a senior administrative person as the project sponsor. The sponsor may take a more active role in the oversight of the project and serve as an advocate/lobbyist/champion for the project within the overall organization. This person would be high enough up to address resource issues and other problems with authority and on a very timely basis.

The project leader will generally have a number of task teams reporting to him or her. These task teams will be responsible for gathering requirements for their areas: bio/demographic information, major prospects, gift processing, alumni relations, technology, or what have you. An experienced leader will head up each task team and be responsible for summarizing needs, ideas, feedback, etc., from his or her area. Leaders as well as other task team members may participate on multiple teams. (See why the steering committee members have to balance priorities?)

The following is a sample project structure.

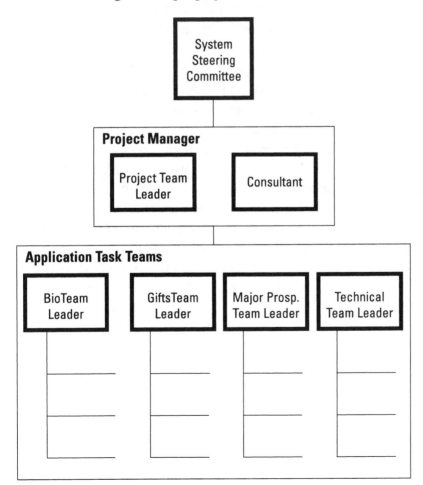

As noted above, many organizations find it beneficial to have a consultant work with the project leader to organize and manage the project. (How do you think we got our experience on hundreds of projects?) Consultants can bring experience with the functional areas, with the process, and with the vendors under consideration. Their experience and skill can expedite the process and reduce the risks inherent in major systems projects.

Staff participation is critical in a project of this nature. First, staff members bring to the table important knowledge of your existing procedures and needs. Second, without their participation and buy-in on the final selection, the implementation is almost guaranteed to fail.

Establishing evaluation criteria

All participants in the selection process believe that their area is the most important part of the development operation. (Don't you want them to believe that?) Without a set of evaluation criteria, your selection decisions will be based on personal preference or perhaps the vote of the person with the most important title. Establishing criteria gives you an objective basis for evaluating vendors and systems. You will be comparing them not only against each other but also against a prioritized list of what's important to your institution.

So what kind of criteria are we talking about? These would include functionality, product flexibility, technology compatibility, vendor support and reliability, ease of use, ability to install on a timely basis, etc. You will identify additional detail for each of these criteria and likely identify some additional criteria that may be unique to your institution and situation.

It's productive to establish weights for each of these criteria to help in quantifying your evaluation. You may note that certain criteria are "go-no go" decisions. For example, one client's selection committee members recently decided that if reference checks pointed out major, unacceptable difficulties in the implementation process, they would discard that vendor system regardless of the weights on other criteria. As they said, "If we can't install the system, what is the value of anything else?"

Note that we haven't included criteria such as vendor track record, productivity enhancement, or costs. If vendors and systems do not meet these criteria, why send them an RFP? They should not even be in the running.

For example, in terms of vendor track record and status in the market, you should consider company size, longevity, financials, stability, etc. What percent of a company's business is in fund-raising software? Is it a sideline or the main business? How many clients are similar in size and need to your institution? If the firm is not a true player, don't even consider it. Furthermore, if its system won't increase your productivity significantly, why consider it? Finally, if you have a $15,000 budget, don't waste your time or that of the vendors with firms that have systems costing $50,000, $100,000, or more.

Confirming the ability to meet your requirements

You must compare vendor responses against your RFP, contact other users, see system demonstrations, and review copies of the system documentation. You must evaluate functional, technical, security, performance, support, and contractual aspects of the vendor's bid and system. You must understand the installation process, including both your responsibilities and the vendor's. You will have to live with and work with the selected system for years; be comfortable in your decision. You will be a partner with the vendor for years; take as much time as you would in choosing a spouse (or more, since love's got nothing to do with this).

Some suggest site visits as a means of making a system decision. Recognize that you'll learn more about the vendor than the system from a site visit. That can be useful, but is it worth the time when a few phone calls can round up virtually the same information?

Nevertheless, do whatever it takes to become satisfied with and committed to your selection decision. Remember the adage that perfection is the enemy of the good. Understand that you won't have perfect knowledge of the vendor or system until perhaps years after you have installed it. Get the best information you can and make your decision.

Your Own Role in Making a Good Choice

An old project management adage goes "Quick, cheap, good—pick two!" This is sometimes translated as "You can't put nine women in a room and expect a baby in a month."

Don't anticipate a good process and system choice if you are not willing to commit adequate resources or enough time. In both the system selection and the subsequent implementation, strive to balance the work to be done (with an acceptable quality level), the resources you have for the project, and a practical time frame.

By following some of the wisdom of this chapter, you can make a successful system's selection. We know. We've done it hundreds of times.

References

"The 1996 Software Guide: Targeting and Reaching the Right Customers More Effectively," *Direct Marketing* 59, no. 2 (June 1996): 34-45.

"1998 Non-Profit Software Guide," *Fund Raising Management* 28, no. 8 (October 1997): 6-16.

Avery, Laura J. and John L. Gliha. "Computer-Assisted Prospect Management and Research," In *Improving Fundraising with Technology: New Directions for Philanthropic Fundraising,* no. 11. San Francisco, CA: Jossey-Bass Publishers, 1996. 85-103.

Baker, Kim and Sunny Baker. "Where Are Your Donors? Getting Up-to-Date with the Latest Mapping Software," *Nonprofit Times* 10, no. 1 (January 1996): 33-34.

Barth, Steve. "Finding a Needle in the Haystack: Use Computer Screening and Database Analysis to Discover the Hidden Major-Gift Prospects Among Your Alumni," CURRENTS 24, no. 6 (June 1998): 32-34, 36-38.

Barth, Steve. "Pulling Gifts Into Your Web: More and More, Campuses are Using Their Web Sites to Cultivate, Solicit, and Steward Gifts, So How's It Working?," CURRENTS 24, no. 8 (September 1998): 32-37.

Bechtold, Ray. "A Specific System for Specific Needs: Like Businesses, Not-for-Profit Organizations Must Measure Incoming and Outgoing Monies—And a Great Deal More. A Fund Accounting System Enables Organizations to Meet Their Particular Fiscal Responsibilities," *Advancing Philanthropy* 5, no. 4 (Winter 1997-1998): 50-51.

Currie, Margaret. "Inside the Harvard Campaign: When You're Running the Largest Fund-Raising Campaign in the History of Higher Education, There's a Lot of Information to Manage. Here's How Harvard University is Using Computer Technology in Its Historic Campaign," *Advancing Philanthropy* 3, no. 4 (Winter 1995): 41-42.

"Cutting Through Today's White Noise: In an Interview with "Advancing Philanthropy," John Groman, Executive Vice President and Chief Creative Officer of Epsilon, Describes the Potential of Computer Technology for Fine-Tuning Messages to Reach Donors Through the Din of Today's Communications Media. Instead of Alienating Donors, Technology Can Help Keep Relationships Strong," *Advancing Philanthropy* 3, no. 4 (Winter 1995): 26-29.

"Cyber-Giving: Corporate Philanthropy on the World Wide Web," *Corporate Giving Watch* 17, no. 8 (October 1997): 1-2.

Gibney, Jean. "Tomorrow's Technologies: Four Ideas That Could Change How Your Office Operates Today or in the Future: Optical Imaging," CURRENTS 23, no. 6 (June 1997): 18-19.

Hall, Holly. "The Pitfalls of 'Screening' Donors" Comparing Data Bases Can Produce a Lot of Information, But Charities Often Don't Know How to Use It," *Chronicle of Philanthropy* 7, no. 13 (April 20, 1995): 26-28.

Hall, Holly. "Technology: Does It Help or Hurt? Charities Need to Rethink How They Use Computers If They Want Machines to Save Them Money," *Chronicle of Philanthropy* 8, no. 11 (March 21, 1996): 39-41.

King, David H. "What Development Professionals Can Learn From Tyrannosaurus Rex," *Fund Raising Management* 28, no. 1 (March 1997): 28-30.

Makley, Bill. "Software for Sale: Here's a Guide for Finding the Leading Purveyors of Grants Management Software and the Key Features of Their Products," *Foundation News and Commentary* 36, no. 54 (September/October 1995): 15-19.

Miller, James D. and Deborah Strauss. *Improving Fundraising with Technology: New Directions for Philanthropic Fundraising*, no. 11. Edited by James D. Miller and Deborah Strauss. San Francisco, CA: Jossey-Bass Publishers, Spring 1996.

Mills-Groninger, Tim. "The Right Tool for the Right Job," In *Improving Fundraising with Technology: New Directions for Philanthropic Fundraising*, no. 11. San Francisco, CA: Jossey-Bass Publishers, 1996. 61-83.

Needleman, Ted. "Donor Management Software: The Nonprofit's Most Important Application?," *Nonprofit Times* 11, no. 13 (September 1997): 23-25.

Needleman, Ted. "Special Report: Fund Accounting Software Still Available Across Platforms," *Nonprofit Times* 11, no. 9 (July 1997): 25-27.

Pollack, Rachel H. "The Road to Software-Buying Success: Computer Pros Who've Both Bought and Sold Alumni-Development Software Tell How to Make an Informed Purchase," CURRENTS 23, no. 5 (May 1997): 36-40.

Ranney, Michael O. "The Implementation of a New System," In *Improving Fundraising with Technology: New Directions for Philanthropic Fundraising*, no. 11. San Francisco, CA: Jossey-Bass Publishers, 1996. 17-28.

Reis, George R. "The 1997 Non-Profit Software Directory," *Fund Raising Management* 27, no. 8 (October 1996): 12-14, 16-22.

Samuel, Tess. "Coming Attractions: Five Trends That Will Affect Prospect Research on the World Wide Web," CURRENTS 23, no. 6 (June 1997): 24-28.

Scheiderman, Martin B. "Setting the Electronic Standard," *Foundation News and Commentary* 37, no. 1 (January/February 1996): 25-27.

Schneiderman, Martin B. "Looking into a New System: When It's Time to Upgrade Your Grants Management Software, You'll Want to Take Advantage of the Newest, Most Efficient Features Available Today. Are These the Items on Your Wish List?," *Foundation News and Commentary* 36, no. 3 (May/June 1995): np.

Strauss, Deborah. "Fundraising and the Superhighway," In *Improving Fundraising with Technology: New Directions for Philanthropic Fundraising,* no. 11. San Francisco, CA: Jossey-Bass Publishers, 1996. 41-59.

Watt, Charles V. "Development Software Requirements Checklist Revised for 1996-97," *Fund Raising Management* 27, no. 8 (October 1996): 32-33.

"What's Where in Software 1997: You Asked for It—Updated Listings of Alumni-Development Computer Systems," CURRENTS 23, no. 5 (May 1997): 42-49.

Chapter 13

More on How to Survive a Computer Conversion

■ By Patricia L. Reynolds
Director of Advancement Services
The Foundation of the State University of New York
at Binghamton

As you've already read in Chapter 12, when it's time to convert to a new or upgraded computer system, the key is planning, planning, planning. Here is still more advice on steps that will enrich your planning and execution at every stage, from pondering the initial decision to sending RFPs.

QUESTIONS TO ASK BEFORE DECIDING TO CONVERT

Either the advancement services director or the database administrator should compile a list of questions to use in evaluating your current system and subsequent office procedures. The most logical questions start with the basics:

- How flexible is your current system in terms of your ability to expand, upgrade, or enhance the software capabilities?
- Does the software provide adequate methods to store infor-

mation for any upcoming capital campaigns? The software should not only be able to track gifts and pledges but also handle research, prospect management, proposals, planned gifts, and stewardship functions.

- Does the system permit automated production of receipts, acknowledgment letters, pledge reminders, solicitation mailings, phonathon cards, donor recognition lists, and reports, reports, reports?
- Are all your computers (desktop and laptop) equipped with sufficient RAM (random access memory), processing speed, and hard-drive capacity to accommodate a new integrated software package?
- Are your computers and printers currently operated through a Local Area Network or mainframe backbone that can provide access to all development and alumni staff who would be using the new software?

After answering the basic questions, it's time to take a more in-depth look at future needs and plan for anticipated growth. Consider some of the more far-reaching questions:

- Does your current system interface readily with other campus systems, such as the admissions and registrar's offices, budget and finance offices, and the personnel office?
- Is your annual fund director planning an automated telemarketing approach?
- Will your annual fund and alumni directors require more specialized segmentation of your alumni population for fund raising, club development, and volunteer involvement in career networks and student recruitment activities?
- Is your administration planning the first, or the next, major capital or comprehensive gift campaign?
- Is your institution moving toward a decentralized or expanded development staff? This requires qualitative as well as quantitative measures of success, especially in the areas of major gifts, corporate and foundation grants, and planned gifts.

MAKING THE CASE

When all signs point to the inevitable, it's prudent to prepare a concise, factual proposal that you can submit to your boss to suggest that it's time to move your organization into the future. This proposal needs to explain all the elements of a conversion, including:

Why: Here you'll use the information you gathered while answering the above questions and evaluating your current system.

Who: It's important to include everyone in every campus office who needs to be part of the conversion process. But begin by recommending that your campus hire an outside consultant who will, at the very least, assist in the requirement-definition and system-selection phases. If your institution will approve it, I recommend hiring a consultant to help in the systems review stage to assess the infrastructure, define systems requirements, make staffing recommendations, and guide conversion planning. A qualified consultant can make the difference between a well-planned, effective conversion and your personal version of "Nightmare on Elm Street."

It's important to include everyone in every campus office who needs to be part of the conversion process.

What: The aforementioned consultant can be helpful in assessing the resources you need for a successful conversion. But your initial proposal should indicate the range of resources required: the software package itself; new/upgraded desk stations for each staff member; network servers or campus network interfaces; training money; additional staff (such as a systems manager, report writer, or other technical support position); consultant fees; and costs associated with product demonstrations, final implementation, and user conferences. The initial proposal will outline what these costs will cover, but actual dollar amounts will not be available until you send out bids and review proposals. The consultant can help provide some rough estimates.

How: Include a basic outline of the steps to conversion. These include retaining a consultant; reviewing all current policies and procedures to help prepare a comprehensive request for bids; and forming task forces and committees to oversee everything from software review and selection to data conversion and final implementation.

When: You can include a tentative timeline with the understanding that you may have to adjust it depending on the advice of the consultant, the complexity of the final system selected, and the availability of staff and resources.

CREATING THE TEAMS YOU'LL NEED

Let's say you've made your case, gotten approvals, and hired the consultant. Now you're fully immersed in Phase I of the conversion project—pulling together the conversion team.

Someone needs to be the project manager or team leader. That will probably be you, if you're the advancement services director. Your institutional makeup will help dictate who else needs to be part of the team. Make sure there's someone related to all critical functions: fund raising, alumni relations, gift processing, research, major gifts, corporate and foundation relations, donor relations, planned gifts, stewardship, file management, budget, computing services, and general administration. As the team leader, you'll be responsible for establishing priorities, assigning tasks, conducting meetings, monitoring progress, and approving all work done on the project.

The conversion team will fall logically into two factions:

1. A steering or oversight committee. This group reviews and evaluates progress on the project, monitors resource allocation, and resolves problems and issues the project team brings forward.

2. The project team. Consisting of members of the user departments, this group will have a wide range of duties, including defining and documenting user needs during the requirements definition phase, assessing vendor proposals during the selection phase, and helping develop procedures and training for all users during the implementation phase.

One of the project team's first objectives should be to form several small subgroups to evaluate current functions and define system requirements that must be part of any new product being considered. Separate groups should focus on:

- biographical data storage and retrieval;
- preparing reports, fund-raising, and phonathon materials;
- processing pledges, gifts, receipts, acknowledgments, and reminders;
- import/export capabilities; and
- data cleanup, deleting, coding, and batch-processing functions.

These task forces will identify the critical functions that must be part of any system you're considering, including any new features or functions that you want but may not be part of the current system. But these new capabilities should also cover every aspect of alumni and development work that anyone has ever asked for or dreamed about. Don't hold back! If you think you might need it, or if you know you would love to have it, include it in the requirements definition phase of your bid proposal. It's better to put in every dream and find out no one can provide it than to leave it off your list and learn after the fact that all you had to do was ask!

THE VENDOR LIST AND RFP

While your task forces are busy compiling their lists of wants and needs, the project leader should work closely with the consultant to identify the most appropriate vendors. Numerous vendors specialize in alumni/development software; you'll find plentiful information on them in their own advertising, brochures, and World Wide Web sites as well as in industry publications. Your consultant can also help you decide which vendors are a good match for the size of your operation, your resources, and your technical environment.

The RFP is crucial because it lets vendors know exactly what you expect from a system.

The lists your task forces come up with will become the basis for the request for proposals you'll submit to your final vendor list. The RFP is crucial because it lets vendors know exactly what you expect from a system. Include every function that your current system readily performs and every data field it conveniently stores. Be sure to list all standard report capabilities that must continue to be part of any replacement system. In addition, incorporate the many new or expanded functions that your task forces suggest adding and other elements that need to be enhanced to meet alumni-development goals during the next several years.

Your RFP should also include a description of the technical environment that houses your current system and the enhancements or changes being considered for a new system. An overview of your operation and its relationship to other campus offices should be part of the introductory portion as well.

If you've hired a consultant, he or she will provide valuable support in preparing the RFP. But if you can't afford a consultant, seek assistance from others at your institution with experience in preparing an RFP. For example, talk to coworkers in such departments as purchasing or computer services. You can also turn to off-campus colleagues who've been through a recent conversion process, search the Internet for any available articles and information, and see the bibliography at the end of Chapter 12.

WHAT TO DO WHILE AWAITING THE PROPOSALS

Vendors need time to prepare their responses to your RFP; plan on about one month. But this doesn't mean your conversion team gets any time off. Not only will this internal project preparation continue while you wait for the proposals to come back, but you'll also find this is an excellent time to outline the next steps in several critical areas:

1. **Conversion plan:** List all areas of preparation, from data cleanup to review of materials; spell out staff members to be involved in the process; and create the projected timetable.

2. **Interfaces:** Outline any desired interfaces with other campus offices, the staff who'll be involved, and the projected timetable.

3. **Procedures:** Review, refine, and redesign all policies and procedures that the new system will affect. Include staff and timetable.

4. **Reports:** Identify current reports and other materials (such as phonathon cards or gift receipts) that must continue to be available. Also get input from appropriate staff members on new reports they'll need, and develop a timetable that reflects when each report needs to be tested and implemented.

5. **Testing:** Establish a specific program for testing each element of the new system to validate procedures, maintain database integrity, verify data entry, and query functions. Include staff and timetable.

6. **Training:** Address all training requirements that will arise from the components of the new system as well as any other software you may need to support that system (such as word-processing, e-mail, or systems applications). Also, list all staff to be trained (everyone from those who do day-to-day data entry to

managers and administrators who will do query or limited input only) and, of course, a training timetable.

THE LAST WORD

It can be daunting to try to plan for the future when you can't even keep pace with the present. But fear not. You are not alone. Those who have forged ahead on other campuses are often willing to share their accomplishments and their challenges with inquiring colleagues who are about to take the plunge. Don't be afraid to ask for advice, input, and support from other advancement services staff who have been through a recent conversion…and survived!

References (see references for Chapter 12)

Chapter 14

Evaluating and Purchasing Support Software: Making a Smart Buy Even When You Know Little About a Program

■ By Kelley Rickard
Assistant Director of Development
Georgetown Preparatory School

Purchasing software that will inevitably become obsolete within six months is a daunting task. But it gets even harder when you have to buy it for a colleague who does a job you don't understand.

Unfortunately, this is a reality for many advancement services professionals. Your coworkers assume you know all there is to know about every related software package. Well, stop right now and raise your hand if you do.

I doubt that you've just dropped this book.

The fact is, there are far too many packages available for alumni administration, planned giving, special events, prospect research, auctions, golf tournaments, etc., for one person, or even one small department, to know all the possibilities. This is especially true if the advancement services staff doesn't work with the programs on a daily or even weekly basis.

You'll be called upon for such buying help anyway. So imagine that you've just received a memo requesting a software package for someone in another department. A few simple steps can make the selection and purchasing process better for everyone. Following the steps is important! Remember, if there is a problem or your colleagues are dissatisfied, they will come to you first.

1. GET THE USER INVOLVED.

This step is first and foremost. Only the user truly knows her job and what the new software is supposed to do. Again, it's a lot to expect of you as an advancement services professional to know the ins and outs of all departments. It's not realistic to assume you know the difference between a bidding frenzy and a silent auction; a NIMCRUT and the gooey stuff in the middle of a candy bar; or an alumnus who pays dues and one who does not.

As part of your learning experience, take the opportunity to find out a little about the department you're purchasing the program for so you can be an educated consumer.

Start by setting up a meeting with the user of the software program. Tell her you'd like to stay in close contact throughout the purchasing process. Ask questions about needs, expectations, computer skill level, department set-up, knowledge of existing programs, and budgetary requirements. Allow and encourage her to ask questions of you.

The first auxiliary software program I purchased was supposed to automate an annual live and silent auction. Never having been to an auction, I didn't know the particulars of what the program should be able to do. Many bumps and bruises later, I found I had spent much more time than necessary to make a simple purchase. The most frustrating part was the number of times I called the same people because I didn't have all of my how, what, and why questions ready at once.

As part of your learning experience, take the opportunity to find out a little about the department you're purchasing the program for so you can be an educated consumer. Ask the user to think of anything about her department that relates directly or indirectly and that could affect things in the long run.

For example, let's say the user is the only planned giving officer. You'll automatically assume you should buy a single-user version of the software. She needs to think to tell you that she's hiring an assistant within six months and wants the software ready when the assistant arrives. Many software programs have vastly different costs depending on the number of users. If you didn't learn this detail in time, her office could face a costly upgrade in six months.

Also enlist the user in sleuthing for information for you. Every area of advancement has an information network. Have the user contact colleagues for software suggestions and the pros and cons of what they use. Just make sure she gathers hard facts. Hearing that a program is difficult to use is not helpful. Hearing that technical support is ineffective because the office only responds to calls from 6 to 9 p.m. is a very good thing to know.

Convince the user that the more information she gathers herself, the more prepared she will be to use the program once it arrives. She needs to feel ownership of the program, since she will be using it.

By now, this question is running through your mind: Why do I have to do so much talking just to purchase a software program? My question back is: Do you want to make the purchase once or multiple times? The more information you arm yourself with in the beginning, the more smoothly the process will go in the end.

2. CONDUCT RESEARCH.

Now that the user is gathering information from her colleagues, it's time to start gathering your own. Where?

- **Listservs.** These are among my favorite sources. As you probably know, a listserv is a virtual environment to which you can send e-mail messages and get responses from others with similar interests. Through these free electronic discussion groups, most advancement professionals are more than willing to share insights. Many times, phone calls from across the country and around the world will ensue. For a project like this, you'll receive names of companies, addresses, phone numbers, Web sites, opinions on whether programs are worth looking at, information on costs and what the demo is like, and more.

For these purposes, one of my favorite listservs is called Fundsvcs (fund services). You can subscribe by going to *lists.duke.edu/archives/fundsvcs.html.*

- **World Wide Web sites.** Using one of the many search engines available on the Web, you can search on the name of a program to find out more information about it. In some cases, you'll locate software manufacturers. In others, you'll find advancement office Web sites that will lead you to a software program. Since the Internet gets new information all the time, don't be surprised if one day you find little information and two weeks later you discover a plethora of material.

- **Your fellow advancement services officers.** Just as you encouraged your user to call on her colleagues, you should contact your own. Many of them have been in your spot, asked to purchase a product they know little about. Gather as much information as you can from trusted sources—and then document all your information. You never know when a colleague will call you for the same advice.

- **The software manufacturers themselves.** Keep the salesperson on the phone as long as necessary to get all your questions answered. Be thorough, and don't be swayed by bells and whistles that only hinder the most necessary functions of the program. Ask what kind of demonstration is available. Try to veer away from a demonstration CD. The demo only shows you what the manufacturer wants you to see in the sequence it designed. Demand a working copy to use with your own data. This is the true test of a software program.

Also ask who the competitors are. Most manufacturers will be more than willing to give out the names of the products they feel are inferior to their own. Then follow up on this information. The competition is not necessarily inferior; it simply offers different capabilities.

3. TAKE THE SOFTWARE FOR A SPIN.

Once you have the program for a demonstration, try it. Install it on the computer it will be used with. Carefully examine the installation process. How easy or difficult is it? Do the directions succinctly guide you through the process? Do the hardware requirements truly satisfy the needs of the program? Are there compatibility issues between the new program and any others the user might have on the computer? Does the program recognize the printer setup the user works with? Software is useless unless it can generate hard copies of material for the user's work.

But don't focus too much on specifics during this first run-through. Simply look at the program's overall layout and workings. Does the package make sense to you? Does anything jump out as inconsistent with the sales brochure?

Make sure you have the right to keep the program on a demonstration basis for a minimum of 30 days.

Try to answer these questions on your own before involving the user. Many times, users are only interested in whether the program works, not how. The time to involve her is when you want to go through the actual program. Both of you should go through the program independently first, and then together. By looking at it separately, you can instinctively recognize components that appear either very good or very bad.

When you sit down with the user at her workstation, judge the program capabilities by using your joint knowledge of the program, how it should work, what it is expected to do, and the general working environment. Ask her questions and do some brainstorming. Combining your general knowledge of advancement services with her specific knowledge of her specialty creates a great opportunity to generate ideas and questions to pose about the software program.

Try the program for various lengths of time and in conjunction with every program the user works with every day. The demonstration period should be as realistic as possible. Use as much of your own data as possible when testing the software. Make sure to use not only representative data but also some unusual cases. You want to be able to measure the scope of the program's ability.

Keep an open line of communication with the technical department during the demonstration period. It's not a good sign if the manufacturer wants to withhold access to technical support. More than likely, it's trying to hide a program flaw if it wants you to deal exclusively with the sales department. On the other hand, many of the support software companies are very small, so the same person might be responsible for technical support and sales. Find out the size of the company you're dealing with and who is responsible for each department.

Make sure you have the right to keep the program on a demonstration basis for a minimum of 30 days. This will give you ample time to work on the program and formulate a multitude of questions and scenarios to apply to it under various working conditions. It will also give you breathing room, so you don't feel as if you have to make a rushed decision. Your institution will be investing a lot of money in the program. You don't want any surprises once you actually own it.

4. MAKE THE PURCHASE.

After all of your trials, research, and questioning, you've decided which software program to buy. This is your final opportunity to make sure the software is compatible with the user's workstation. Ask what format the program will come in. Do you have the proper driver to install the full program? Can the program be downloaded from the Internet? Do you have to install the program during the manufacturer's business hours for special passwords during the installation? There are always problems that come up at the last minute. Make as many preparations as possible to avoid the pitfalls.

Discuss with the user exactly when she needs the program. Many smaller companies will periodically offer specials. This could lead to significant savings and allow the user to purchase the extra RAM that would make the program really sing.

Make sure you get in writing what's included with the purchase. Are you entitled to any maintenance agreement, or does this cost extra? Such agreements are well worth the cost; most companies include free upgrades along with tech support if you purchase the maintenance agreement.

Is the technical support limited or unlimited, or is there an option? Talk to the user. Her comfort level with the program, and with computers in general, should determine the amount of tech support you need to buy. Also ask if the same amount needs to be purchased year after year. A variable plan might be good if the user is indeed planning to hire another person in six months who will need additional tech support.

Now's the time to look into training options for the user. You might be able to get a cheap training rate if you pay for it with the purchase. However, training usually has a time limit, so be aware of the user's schedule. If the training is free, it might be interesting for you to participate also. Just be careful that the user doesn't then depend solely on you to answer all of her questions. This is a risk you need to weigh for yourself.

I always suggest working with a program for at least a couple of weeks before attending a training program. This lets the user learn the program's day-to-day operation before being inundated with higher-level information.

5. LAY THE GROUNDWORK FOR THE FUTURE.

Once you've installed the program, it's time to set ground rules on everything the user should and can expect from you. Speak up now or problems could arise down the road. The user might assume that since you purchased the software, you are now an expert and will help her make it work. So whom should she go to with program problems, printing problems, and emergency technical problems on the night of an event or during a meeting with a constituent?

> *I always suggest working with a program for at least a couple of weeks before attending a training program.*

If you feel your workday is full enough as it stands, then speak up now. Have the user learn to rely on the manufacturer's tech, who should be able to handle her problems quickly and efficiently. In the meantime, you'll be able to move on to other issues, like purchasing that new program to link the development office with alumni relations.

Of course, if you work in a small office the way I do, you might have to learn how the program works for practical reasons. For example, if the user leaves your institution, someone will need to train the new employee, and if budgetary constraints keep you from outsourcing the training, you'll need the expertise. Also, for many support software programs, technical support is limited to regular business hours, Monday through Friday. We've all suffered through a disastrous software crash when we were working late on a project for an important meeting the next day. In rare cases like this, the user should be able to turn to you for assistance.

But whatever course of action you choose, make sure it suits your needs. Do not take on more responsibility than you can handle. Otherwise you may end up working in several different areas you've purchased software for. Is this what you want?

Purchasing software for others gives you the chance to expand your own knowledge even as you help integrate advancement services into the rest of the advancement department. Many people feel intimidated when shopping for technology. Your support and understanding will give your colleagues confidence in their own ability to recognize a good buy—and the skill.

Chapter 15

Strategies for Linking Your Database with Your Web Site

■ By Brian Dowling
Associate Vice President of Marketing and Advancement Services
Colorado School of Mines
(Former Director of Advancement Services at California State
University, Fresno)

As thousands of new World Wide Web sites come online every week, Internet traffic is growing at an incredible rate. No wonder. The Web is interactive, which makes it great for exchanging information directly, and it contains lots of dynamic content that visitors can relate to personally.

These same traits make the Web an important link between your campus and your constituents. Because a substantial amount of your Web content probably resides in your database, you can now merge your database with Web technologies to enhance your outreach activities. This is an exciting time for you in advancement services. By using your extensive knowledge of the Internet, networking, and database technologies, you can participate directly in marketing your campus.

MARKETING YOUR INSTITUTION WITH YOUR DATABASE

Your advancement database is a valuable asset without which your advancement programs would be impossible to manage.

Think of all a database accomplishes. You do mailings and include salutations in the merge letter so appeals are more personal. You produce annual reports, honor rolls of donors, and lists of alumni receiving awards. You collect and record e-mail and home page addresses. You send out birthday cards, reunion invitations, and letters from the president. You keep track of trustees, chapter presidents, emeritus professors, community leaders, and volunteer service records.

> *There are only two limits to what you can feature on your Web site: what you have stored in your database, and your imagination.*

Now you can help market your institution to your external constituents by putting much of this same information on your Web site. Honor rolls, board membership lists, project founders, and much more can be extracted and displayed there. If you set up your connection correctly, you don't even have to update your Web pages manually every time you receive data changes.

The Web is also effective for distributing information to your internal users. They don't have to be logged into your network to run reports. They don't have to request a run from your programmer/analyst or research staff. When advancement staff members need reports from the road, they can dial up a local Internet service provider, open their browser, click on a link, and analyze their data immediately. Similarly, volunteers can review changes in campaign organization charts from wherever they access the Internet. This easy access lets you eliminate a lot of printing and distribution of information. And since data for the Web comes directly from your database, it's as up-to-date as your last processed and posted batch, your last biographical update, or the last change in your prospect management system.

There are only two limits to what you can feature on your Web site: what you have stored in your database, and your imagination.

THINKING CREATIVELY ABOUT USING YOUR DATABASE

To come up with new ideas, you need to change the way you view documents, brochures, reports, invitations, and other hard-copy materials. Always ask, How can we improve our marketing pieces by combining our database and the Internet?

For example, after sending out reunion invitations, you can create a Web page that dynamically displays the list of people who've accepted—a sure way to increase interest in the event. You can create attendance lists from the past that include anecdotes from previous reunions.

By displaying scholarship recipients on a scholarship page, you can show donors who benefited from their contributions. And as a resource for new or prospective members, student and constituent alumni associations can post online membership rosters and lists of their officers, complete with contact information.

To get all your colleagues to think of new approaches in a new medium, your campus may need to reorganize its traditional creative departments and processes. Consider adding a writer position to the campus Web technology group, including the campus Webmaster on the publications committee, or having your advancement database programmer work directly with your Web site design consultants.

As part of this, all staff members need to take every opportunity to tell constituents about your Web site and—more important—to make sure they'll find interesting information when they get there. Gift acknowledgements can include the line "See our donor honor roll on our Web site." Travel brochures can say, "Visit our Web site to see who's traveling with you on this trip." Phonathon scripts can include the line, "Check your reunion class's giving totals and see how they compare to others' at our Web site."

COSTS AND BENEFITS OF A WEB/DATABASE PROJECT

Traditional cost/benefit analysis may not apply to a Web/database project. Obviously, it requires up-front investments in technology and training, but payback may not be immediate if site traffic builds only gradually.

That's why it's better to follow a longer-term investment/return strategy than to seek a one-time expense allocation. You should position a Web/database project as an integral component of the budget process and then obtain recurring or core funding. Just don't forget to include ongoing maintenance and development. After creating your first Web/database pages, you will have lots of ideas for more.

While making the case for budget, remember these considerations.

- **To a large degree, the hardware, software, and staff you already have will determine your project costs.** So evaluate these carefully before submitting your budget request to uncover hidden costs and generate ideas to reduce expenses.

  For example, everyone who has a database is already maintaining it and extracting information. It's relatively simple to modify existing reports for Web deployment; you just need some software to interface your Web server with your database. However, you may have to upgrade to a faster server. If you work in a centralized mainframe shop, your costs will be different than in a departmental server environment.

- **The skill of your technical staff is also critical to your success.** If you lack in-house expertise, you will need to invest in training or look outside.

  One possibility is to work with a directory publishing company or Internet service provider that develops online communities. (The publishing company route would be especially good if your campus happens to be doing an alumni directory right now.) This way, you can begin to use your data as you benefit from the vendor's technical experience. These vendors set up pages on your Web site using your data. Visitors can access and update addresses, exchange employment and career information, network with alumni who have similar interests, and participate in other interactive data-related pursuits.

- **Your project will be more affordable if you make creative use of your resources.** To help reduce costs, work with your advancement database vendor as a guinea pig site on developing Web/database applications. Have student interns help develop your site so they can receive credit for a database-related course. Involve students you already employ if they're interested in learning Web technology. Such partnerships lower costs and help share technical knowledge.

- **As you tally your costs, don't forget the money-saving benefits.** For example, posting an honor roll makes it available to a larger audience and reduces the number of printed copies. The price of printing and distributing in-house reports goes down when staff can access and run them with a browser. By putting an expanded class notes section online, your magazine has the ability to add more detail to this popular section and attract more readers without adding more printing costs.

> *Because Internet technology is a fast-moving target, it's difficult to determine the optimal technical infrastructure for a Web/database project.*

Web data deployment also reduces Web page maintenance. As you add more names to a list of distinguished alumni award winners, you just add the record in your database and it also appears on the Web. Online e-mail and home page directories, with their thousands of entries, are much easier to update as well.

You already use your data in reports, for events, in your alumni magazine, and as part of your annual report. Using it on the Web leverages your data acquisition and maintenance activities. It's an easy and effective way to reduce the ratio of data ownership costs to data use costs.

TECHNICAL INFRASTRUCTURE AND DATA DESIGN CONSIDERATIONS

Because Internet technology is a fast-moving target, it's difficult to determine the optimal technical infrastructure for a Web/database project. Try to use tools you already have. Support and expertise are easier to find for common hardware and software standards.

It's essential to develop a Web data warehouse. The warehouse will contain extraction tables with pre-formatted data updated via nightly, weekly, or monthly routines. Because of efficiency issues, Web extraction tables require a different architecture from a conventional fund-raising database. Sorting, name formatting, totaling, and similar CPU/IO-intensive tasks should be done on the server and saved in extraction tables. A good rule of thumb is to separate the data extraction from the presentation on the client. Use indexes, summary tables with a minimum number of rows, and flat files, and limit the number of "joins" or

> *Throughout the technical and design process, your advancement database vendor should be an integral part of your effort.*

instances when you join two sets of data using a common denominator. Do everything you can to minimize processing when Web pages are called up so they are served quickly to the visitor's machine.

Remember to test your results with different browsers, on different client machines, and using a dial-up connection. Record page-loading times and work to reduce them. Server loads can increase dramatically when visitors access reports on a regular basis. Heavily trafficked sites may need a separate Web reporting database and server.

Throughout the technical and design process, your advancement database vendor should be an integral part of your effort. The vendor should constantly enhance its product to make data deployment on the Web easier, both operationally and technically. For example, there should be tables that contain fields for e-mail addresses and URLs, and "permission to use on the Web" flags that can be set in these and other tables.

The software your vendor provides should be able to extract and display data on Web pages. Some of this software should enable you to use Web forms so visitors can input data and submit it directly to your database tables. You should also be able to get comprehensive statistics showing the IP (Internet Protocol) address of the visitor, and what, when, and how data were accessed. Such information is important for ongoing planning and development.

All of these features need to be included in your vendor's base package and a major component of its design philosophy. If your vendor doesn't offer these facilities, but rather presents them as expensive custom or add-on solutions, you may need to consider another product.

Here are a couple of final points to remember: The way you set up your data for access is very important. Consider where information will be extracted from, how it will be extracted, and how much time it takes. You'll lose a lot of visitors if they click on a link and have to wait more than a few seconds for a response.

Also, the data you display on the Web may be different than in printed media. So think about dual-deployment issues when you design a data extraction. For example, an in-house honor roll report may include total giving for each donor, whereas a Web version may have names only, grouped within giving societies.

DATA COLLECTION AND DATA VIGILANCE

If you want your Web/database project to be more effective, you should both add to the types of data you collect and enhance your data-collection procedures.

- **What to collect.** Several new data elements can help you now or in the future. So during your annual fund or membership drive, you might consider asking for your constituents' e-mail addresses. Or start collecting a mother's maiden name or other unique identifier your constituents can use as a password when they're looking up and updating their own information. For other ideas, ask visitors what data-related features they'd like to see added to your site.

As part of this, think about how new data elements can help your marketing activities. For example: Let's say class notes are added to your database. Then they're extracted and dynamically displayed on your Web site. Then they're merged into your alumni magazine. You're using the same data in separate marketing pieces but maintaining it only once. You're also building an anecdotal history of constituents for your research staff. If you collect class notes via a form on your Web site, you have even conveyed data ownership to your visitors. This will make them more inclined to return to update their accomplishments and see what others have done. Collecting and displaying the right data can significantly enlarge your target audience.

Additional examples of data you may want to collect are current employment, professional associations, and hob-

How Can You Learn More about the Technical Side?

Your central technology staff can be a great information source. Ask what products staffers use and if they have site licenses. Participate in on-site training classes. Access news groups and listservs, and subscribe to Internet-related publications. Learn the buzzwords.

Network with peer institutions that have online communities as well as with others who use their data on the Web. Ask them about pitfalls, hurdles, benefits, and the best and worst technology they've invested in. Spend time reviewing their sites. Get comparative statistics on database size, site traffic, hardware configurations, and staffing. Try to estimate how much extra maintenance and support they needed for a Web/database project once it was initiated. All this will help you immensely on your own projects.

bies. You can use these categories to create Web pages through which visitors can network with others who have similar interests. Constituents can volunteer as mentors or as resources for an "ask an expert" page. Visitors add their names to an e-mail directory and return to see who else is listed. As you add more e-mail addresses to your database, the page becomes a better resource. And later, you can use the e-mail addresses to distribute electronic newsletters.

- **The importance of data vigilance.** You must double-check every Web/database report you create for completeness and accuracy. This is especially important given the natural tendency to post a Web page and not look back at it for some time. If you put up the wrong year for a past alumni president's term, many more people may end up seeing this over time than would see a static report.

    The same attention to detail is necessary with information that visitors submit. Always edit for spelling and grammatical errors. Check class years and degree information against what you have on file and resolve any differences. When information is submitted directly, you should store it temporarily in a "holding table" and review it before it's transferred to "live" tables.

SECURITY ISSUES AND PERMISSIONS

Make special security plans for two types of data you'll be deploying: private data restricted to specific visitors, and public data available to all visitors.

- **Private data.** Server security programs that manage directory, folder, and file permissions are usually sufficient to control access to private data. You can create password-protected pages to run private reports and to access confidential information, such as nightly annual fund totals. If your internal audience is large enough, create a separate Web site and house this information on its own server. This makes security management much easier.
- **Public data.** These need to be accessible. Perform tests from off campus to make sure firewalls are not locking visitors out—a problem that might not be obvious when you test on your own network segment. Test with anonymous log-

ins to verify that your database engine's security is allowing visitors to extract and view information.

More complicated security issues arise with pages such as "contact an alumni expert," which display name and contact information. One solution is to create a separate registration Web page. This Web page will require users to submit specific information so you can verify who is sending data. You can limit who views these pages by assigning specific permissions and passwords. Use site certificates to secure and encrypt transmissions. From a maintenance standpoint, you have to balance comprehensive data availability with your ability to manage security.

To verify data submissions from visitors, send e-mails confirming that their data have been added. Let them know the URL where the additions are displayed and ask them to review the information and inform you if there are additional changes. Not only is this a good double-check, but it also gives them a second chance to rescind permission if they change their minds about displaying their data.

Visitors can download information displayed on a page, so don't create pages that provide too much information. If you include complete addresses, they can create mailing lists. Never display sensitive or specific identifiers such as social security numbers unless they are password-protected and restricted to specific individuals or groups.

> *To allay security fears about not-so-sensitive information, remind visitors that the people who go to your Web site are similar to those who read your publications.*

In contrast to printed publications directed to targeted groups, Web pages are available to anyone with a computer. This can increase fears about displaying personal information. Your data-collection vehicles should include language to the effect that "Your data may be used for institutionally approved marketing programs, including our Web site. Contact <name of person> if you don't want this used." In addition, place permission checkboxes on electronic data-collection forms. Ask for very explicit permission to display contact information like addresses. Database tables should have appropriate flags set to exclude those who request anonymity.

Your institution's publicity rules should also apply to the Web. Release forms need to include Internet-related language. Whenever you develop a Web data extraction, review it carefully to ensure that constituents who have asked to be excluded are not displayed.

To allay security fears about not-so-sensitive information, remind visitors that the people who go to your Web site are similar to those who read your publications. In fact, alumni magazines or annual reports sent to your complete mailing list might well have larger audiences than your Web site. At the same time that you don't want to make personal information publicly available, you don't want to be so fearful about small security risks that you fail to make your site as interesting as possible.

SUCCESS STORIES AND THE FUTURE

The fact is, linking your database with the Web can be one of your most important additions to the array of services you provide to your institution.

In 1997-98, when I worked at California State University, Fresno, we set up about 50 reports that accessed our advancement database on our advancement Web site (129.8.21.20). These included a list of everyone with a birthday today, class notes, a look-up-by-last-name feature that let visitors see if the university considered them lost, chapter membership listings, 50-year graduates, and more. In the first year, our reports were accessed over 75,000 times. In the aggregate, they continue to be one of the highest-traffic areas on the site.

Integrating Web sites and databases will be instrumental in creating a more positive online experience.

The results were gratifying. We received many compliments about the fact that this information is available. We reduced the number of internally run reports. We received thousands of information updates. We found that alumni submit and view their class notes online. We also reduced maintenance on our alumni excellence award winners, association past presidents, emeriti professors, faculty staff listings, and other pages.

Other institutions that use their databases on the Web could probably tell similar success stories, as is evidenced by the growth in the number of online communities containing interactive data-related activities.

I predict that the Web will continue to become more important as a primary contact point. Bandwidth improvements will facilitate easier access to data, pictures, sound, and video. We'll see more customization of presentation based on visitor preferences, and it will become commonplace for visitors to find extensive data of personal interest. Web sites will become more inter-active and interesting. Competition to attract visitors, hold their interest, and induce them to return will become more intense as ease of access makes the Web more like such conventional enter-tainment media as radio and television.

Integrating Web sites and databases will be instrumental in creating a more positive online experience. Constituents will look up and correct their biographical data, review and print out their giving records, network with experts in their field, find lost friends, locate people with similar interests, leave multi-media messages, and much, much more. That's why it's a good time to get started on your first Web/database project.

Chapter 16

Document Imaging 101:
Going Paperless Without Pain

■ By John Ley
*IMPACT Project Co-Lead (PeopleSoft Advancement
Implementation), Southern Methodist University
(Formerly Manager of Gift Accounting and Campaign Reporting,
SMU)*

First, a question: What do worms, jukeboxes, and Mars all have in common? This chapter will cover the answer to this and much more.

Next, an observation. Even if you don't realize it, by the time you've started reading this, you've undoubtedly already considered several options for what's known by the fancy name of "records management." The most common option is, of course, storing paper documents in file cabinets. Another possibility is microfilm and microfiche, which give you a space-saving way to archive infrequently used records that you nevertheless need to save for historical purposes.

But recently, another method of records management has emerged: document imaging. This process stores records in an electronic format. But unlike a database that collects words and figures electronically, document imaging actually stores graphics. In essence, the result is a photocopy that you can view on your computer monitor or print on your printer.

Finally, a hint. In this chapter we'll briefly address alternative records-management systems, but our major focus will be on document imaging. Topics will include how document imaging works, what its pros and cons are, who in your office should use it, and why. By the time we're done, you'll not only know about worms, jukeboxes, and Mars, but you'll also understand how to justify and implement a document-imaging system.

HOW DOCUMENT IMAGING WORKS

There are four basic components of a document imaging system, with one possible (and recommended!) bonus component. These four components correspond with the primary functions you perform when storing and retrieving records; the bonus is OCR, or optical character recognition. Here's a basic summary of the four components.

1. **Scanning.** Think of this as making an electronic photocopy of a document. To do it, you need a scanner, a piece of computer equipment that "takes a picture" of documents, and document-imaging software, which links your computer to the scanner. The process is fairly simple. Generally, as you scan a document, the image appears on your monitor. You can then review the image quality to make sure it will be readable when you retrieve it, either from your monitor or as a printout. Most imaging software lets you adjust for size, clarity, brightness, etc. When you're happy with the image, a simple click of a button accepts the image and gets you ready for the next step.

2. **Coding.** This process tells the system where the document is located—somewhat like describing which file cabinet and file folder a document is in. Generally, with document imaging software, when you have the document displayed on your monitor, a separate window displays a number of fields you can choose from to describe the document. Ideally, you can custom-design this window for your own institution. If not, you should at least be able to modify it somewhat to fit your specific needs. At a minimum, you'll want to code in constituent name, ID number, title and type of the document you're coding, and document date.

Other fields you may elect include type of constituent as categorized by the Council for Aid to Education; campaign with which the document is affiliated; area of campus with which it's affiliated; purpose code; author of document; scanner of document; or a free text field that gives you additional space to record specific information about the particular document. The possibilities are endless. It's well worth your time to make this coding screen as useful as possible. The benefits will be obvious whenever you try to retrieve similar documents. We'll cover additional benefits (and drawbacks) a bit later.

3. **Archiving**. This is the process of permanently storing documents for later use. In most cases, document-imaging systems store documents on an optical disk also referred to as a WORM, which stands for Write Once, Read Many. This means that although you only have to record the information once, it can be read an unlimited number of times.

What makes an optical disk unique is that the recorded image and coding are considered permanent. You can add pages to the document, update the coding, or even take away pages from the initial view, but the original document cannot be changed. New versions are recorded as revisions; previous versions are stored in the "background," and you can view them if desired. One of the benefits to saving previous versions is that the entire document, beginning to end, is recognized as permanent. It was once said that such a disk is so immutable that it would be admissible as evidence in a court of law. If that's ever an issue for you, ask your campus legal counsel for confirmation.

An important note: Keep in mind that even though we've explained how you would conduct the process up to this point on a single document, it's common to scan many documents at once, code them at your leisure, and archive them in batches. The procedure is not that different from copying and filing papers in large quantities.

4. **Retrieving**. This is a document imaging system's big payoff. You can search by any of the criteria you chose during the coding phase. To see a constituent's entire file, just tell the system to search on the particular name or ID number and the list of documents will appear. To narrow down the number of "hits" you get, simply indicate more criteria. For example, you could essentially tell the system to search for all documents with a particular ID number that are coded as gifts given between June and August of last year.

Ideally, your document-imaging system will assign a system-generated number to each scanned document. This saves time because you needn't search through various constituents' records or multiple documents. For example, if your colleagues are looking for a contact report from the visit between your president and Mr. and Mrs. Major Donor last November, you can tell them it's Log No. 123,456 on the document-imaging system. They can then call up that particular log number at their desks and read the report. No searching through files, no photocopying papers, no waiting for something to arrive via campus mail. That's how document imaging saves time, paper, and money.

A BRIEF LOOK AT THE BONUS FUNCTION, OCR

With normal retrieval, you search for a document based on the information inputted during coding. With optical character recognition, the system actually reads the document so that you can search on specific words or phrases. This can be a powerful tool for prospect researchers and others. But as you can imagine, the process is complicated. Just how much can be read depends on your documents' legibility and your particular product's sophistication. Some OCR products can read handwriting, but most deal with the typewritten word.

The ability to scan documents and search through them for key words is something that will greatly enhance your prospect research efforts.

Another feature a document imaging system may have is called a computer-originated document, or COD. Normally, you would print a document, scan it, code it, and archive it. But with COD, a document you created in your word-processing or spreadsheet program would not have to be printed. You'd simply code it and archive it in its electronic format from your desktop. The benefit is that you skip a step and save paper. The drawback is that to retrieve the document, the specific application that created it must be available on the computer you're using. In an age of ever-changing software, this may be a problem. But it's well worth investigating to see if this feature would benefit your institution.

Not all document imaging systems come with OCR, although it's growing more popular. Although it costs more and certainly requires more planning and coordination, OCR can be worth the extra effort. The ability to scan documents and search through them for key words is something that will greatly enhance your prospect research efforts.

WHO USES DOCUMENT IMAGING?

The answer to this question should be a resounding, "Everybody!" Remember that we're talking about a records-management system. When an office uses multiple systems for the same function, complications arise concerning access, availability, and maintenance. To have information available to all who need it, everyone should use the same system.

Essentially, there are two types of users: the power user and the casual user. You should tailor your training to accommodate the needs and interests of each.

More significant are the two directions from which your staff will use the system: input and output. Primary input areas include gift accounting, constituent records, alumni relations, administration and support, public affairs, and various other offices. Primary output areas include prospect research, fund raising, and various other offices.

In theory, everyone should be able to put documents into the system and then retrieve them. Granted, there is overlap in many of these areas, but in practice, the functions tend to be divided. Recognizing this will aid in training, but more important, it will aid in determining how you want the system designed. You should encourage all users to give input on your document imaging system's design.

DA GOODS, DA BADS, AND DA UGLIES!

Almost everything we do has benefits and drawbacks, and using a document-imaging system is no exception. The benefits are obvious: The system allows you to save file space. It alleviates most access problems, since from your desktop, you can call up any document to which you have security access. It saves time, since you won't have to go to a records-storage area to retrieve the desired document, and it may also save paper, since you may not have to print so many documents.

The drawbacks are the same ones you'd have with your current system, any new system, or any electronic system. These include lost and mis-filed documents, the need for somewhat specialized training, and the reliability of your network or computer structure.

The challenge is to meet these potential drawbacks head on and develop plans to overcome them before problems arise. Lost and mis-filed documents are a product of poor training and follow-up. To alleviate this, emphasize two areas.

First, know the particular document. Let's say a fund raiser writes a letter to a particular constituent, but the person who scans and codes the document doesn't understand it and codes it to a different constituent. Naturally, it will never show up when the correct constituent's record is searched. To address this problem, have all people who create a document scan and code it. If this isn't always practical or optimal, create a coding form that has the same information on it that the coding screen does. The author or creator of the document can fill out the form and clip it to the original document, thus allowing the scanning person to code the document correctly. (For examples of two coding forms, one long and one short, see Appendices A and B at the end of this chapter.)

Second, insist on proper scanning. There are levels of quality in scanning just as there are in photocopying. Whoever is doing the work should conduct a thorough review of the scanned image before archiving it and disposing of the original. Proper training and quality control are key.

As mentioned earlier, a major challenge is making sure that everyone uses the same records-management system. Make a plan for old files as well as new documents. For maximum productivity, all documents should be available on the document-imaging system.

Using your system to the fullest requires participation, buy-in, communication, and training. Again, to get buy-in and ensure that the system does what it should, you need to involve all departments in the decision-making process. Constant communication keeps fear of the new to a minimum while making users feel involved.

How Do You Justify a Document-imaging System?

uestions you should definitely consider include, Do we really need document imaging? How will it make our life easier? Can we afford *not* to get it? Will it raise more money? This last question tends to be the ultimate one whenever you evaluate large expenditures. It's not an easy question to answer.

Thinking through the reasons why you're considering a change may make finding the answers less difficult, however. Justifications include both access and space concerns, but space concerns have a cost factor attached that's very tangible and can be used to make your case.

In 1993, Southern Methodist University, conducted a study of the cost of our records management system. The following is a brief summary of what we found.

Proposal and Cost Justification

Current records-storage situation (physical and cost):

- 80 file cabinets, vertical and lateral
- 100,000 constituent files
- 1,400 square feet—15 percent of usable floor space
- 3 more file cabinets added annually

Costs (first year of five-year timeframe):

File cabinets:	$ 2,000
Input costs (personnel):	136,000
Retrieval costs (personnel):	126,000
Retrieval cost (mis-filed docs):	50,000
Storage costs:	0
Photocopies:	16,000
Total:	$ 330,000
Estimated cost in fifth year:	$ 720,000

Solution: Document Imaging

Using the same factors listed above, we found that if we bought a document-imaging system, we could project cost savings within two years. This was due to spending less time and money on inputting, retrieving, and finding mis-filed documents as well as needing less space for document storage.

In figuring the above costs, we used the following statistics, which we determined through intensive surveys of all employees who performed the indicated tasks.

Minutes per document to index and file:	10	Hourly rate of executives/professionals	$ 19.44
Minutes per document to find and retrieve:	15	Percent burden	33%
Minutes per document to find mis-filed docs:	60	Average rate of payroll increases	4%
Percent docs retrieved by professionals/execs:	60%	Number of photocopies per year	100,000
Percent docs mis-filed:	10%	Cost per page (including labor)	$ 0.15
Hourly rate of documents filers	$ 9.44	Percent annual growth per year	10%
Hourly rate of document retrievers	$ 19.44		

This analysis proved successful. Management approved our imaging system, which we've been using ever since.

HOW DO YOU IMPLEMENT A DOCUMENT-IMAGING SYSTEM?

B y the time you reach the point of implementation planning, you have presumably researched the products available and determined which is best for you. You have also examined integration needs and opportunities with your current systems, upgrade potential, vendor service reputation, equipment needs, costs, and so on.

Now it's time to make your system work for you.

It's vital to spend adequate time on planning and designing your implementation. During that process, the questions you need to ask and decisions you need to make fall into these categories.

- **Coding.** What information do you use to code your documents? What fields are required? What fields are optional? Is there such a thing as requiring too many fields? Will fewer fields speed up data entry but slow down retrieval? Getting input from both the people who'll be coding and scanning documents and those who'll be the primary document retrievers is extremely important.

    In most cases, but not all, an advancement office may consider only donor files. What about nondonor files? What about files that relate to particular projects, such as scholarship recognition dinners—how are those files coded? Do you assign a project number rather than a computer ID number? What about standard office files—do you assign a departmental number? How are those coded for retrieval? A standard format policy is something to think about before people start using the system. (See Appendix C for an example of SMU's policy.)

- **Scanning policies.** What do you do with your old and current files? Do you have the resources to scan and code existing files? Do you store them off-site and begin scanning only new information? Or do you pull certain files for scanning? Addressing questions like these up front will save time and money down the road. Be very realistic about what you'll need to accomplish the goals you've set.

    What records will you scan? Is there anything that is too confidential? If so, where are these records stored? Who has access, and how do they know where to find them? Why are these records considered too confidential? Why would a document that is too confidential be created to begin with? Be careful not to fall into the trap of having to maintain multiple records management systems. Remember, sharing information enables the advancement office to do its job best.

- **Access.** Who has what access? Do you have various levels of it? Do those who work in advancement on other parts of your campus have access? Who monitors this? Who decides who has access?

- **Getting the work done.** Who scans the documents? Who codes them? Who does the scanning of old files? Who does the scanning of current files and records? Is this responsibility centralized, or does everyone share the job? Who does your current filing? Do you hire temporary workers to scan old files? Who trains them and monitors their work?

- **Organizing your system.** How will your optical disks be labeled? An optical disk holds a great deal of information, but it does fill up. How will you label multiple disks? Do you try to put certain types of information on certain disks or just put information in chronological order?

- **System training.** Who will do what training? Do you have a special training group? Is it your computer department? Your records department? Both?

- **Quality control.** What type of quality control process will you have in place? Who does it? Who corrects errors that are found? Quality control takes valuable time that no one wants to put forth, but in the long run will pay off in important ways.

- **Overall management.** How will document imaging integrate into your current system(s) and procedures? Is it a separate task, or should you work it into your current workflow? Does your gift-processing area work from copies of checks or scan the checks prior to depositing? Or do you scan checks at all?

ADDITIONAL EQUIPMENT NEEDS

Depending on your current computer structure, you may or may not have to buy new equipment. If your general users have up-to-date computers that meet your document-imaging vendor's specifications, you shouldn't require any upgrading. Remember that you can view documents from any workstation that has the document-imaging software.

In order to scan documents, you obviously need a scanner. But it could be overkill—and overly expensive—to have scanners at each employee's workstation. A perfectly good configuration would have a scanning station in each area. In such a case, the scanning station would be dedicated to scanning while the coding of documents could take place at the staff's regular workstations.

In addition to scanners, a document-imaging system will need its own servers and disk readers. The type and number of servers will depend on your particular system and its specifications. The optical disks, or worms, are stored in a server referred to as a jukebox. It's called that because it acts like a record-playing jukebox, retrieving and inserting optical disks into the readers as the user requests them.

AND, OH YES . . .

What *do* worms, jukeboxes, and Mars all have in common? We've already established that a worm is an optical disk that stores information. A jukebox is the server that houses the worms. And Mars? Mars® happens to be the document-imaging system SMU purchased from Micro Dynamics in 1993. (It's now owned by Docucorp.) MARS stands for Multi-User Archival and Retrieval System, and it includes both worms and jukeboxes.

Clearly, a document-imaging system is a powerful tool. In these days of information overload and lightening-fast response, an imaging system is just one more means to meet the demands placed on your advancement office. With proper planning, implementation, and training, it can be a great complement to your overall information management system.

Appendix A

Document Coding Form (Long)

CID/POS/PROJ#: _____

(If no CID exists, please complete CID Request Form in Request Folder on Server)

(CID= Donor Related files, POS= non-Donor, office files, PROJ= Assigned Project Code)

Last Name/Org. Name: _____

First Name, etc., (Individuals Only) _____

Document Title: _____ ---- _____
     Doc Type

Document Date: _____

Long Document
     Date: _____

Document Type (check one):

__ Acknowledgment Letter (ACK)
__ Annuity Agreement (ANN)
__ News Clip (CLP)
__ Contact Report (CON)
__ Correspondence (COR)
__ Endowment Agreement (END)
__ Gift (GF)
__ Gift with Letter (GFL)
__ Inter-Office Memo (MEMO)
__ Pledge (PL)
__ Pledge with Letter (PLL)
__ Profile (PRF)
__ Proposal (PRP)
__ Payment (PY)
__ Payment with Letter (PYL)
__ Research Information (RINF)
__ Stewardship Report (STRP)
__ Trust Agreement (TRU)
__ Other (OTH)

SMU Author (if applicable):

_____

Access: _____

Campaign (check one):
__ None   __ TDA   __ 3GE
__ CAP   __ Annual   __ Other

Area (check up to six):
__ None   __ Law
__ Athletics   __ Meadows (Arts)
__ Cox (Business)   __ Perkins (Theology)
__ Dedman College   __ Science & Engineering
__ General University   __ Other

Purpose (if applicable):
__ None   __ Research
__ Unrestricted   __ Library
__ Other Restricted   __ Physical Plant
__ Prop. Bldg. & Equip   __ Student Financial Aid
__ End. Restricted   __ Academic
__ End. Unrestricted   __ Office Stuff
__ Faculty/Staff   __ Other

Is this a revision of a document previously scanned?
          ____ Yes   ____ No

Please list up to three KEYWORDS / BRIEF
PHRASES for future searches (NOT REQUIRED):

_____
_____
_____

Submitted by: _____   Date: _____

Appendix B

Document Coding Form (Short)

(reduced to fit on a half-sheet of paper)

To Be Scanned/Re-Coded

Log # _____ Dev. _____

Originator_____

                                                Date

_____ New?

_____ Insert? (add to beginning of document)

_____ Append? (add to end of document)

_____ Rescan? (replace page of document)

Need to be coded/re-coded? YES NO

(Indicate ONLY what needs to be changed or added)

CID_____

FIRST NAME_____

LAST NAME_____

TITLE_____

DATE_____

DOC TYPE_____

CAMPAIGN_____

AMOUNT_____

MR#_____

Appendix C

Coding Policy for Nondonor Files

Southern Methodist University

Development Policy for Coding of Project Files and Documents

All documents fall into one of three categories:

1. **Constituent files:** These should already have a CID assigned to them. If not, one should be assigned to them.
2. **Inner-office files:** Items that are related specifically to a position and are not related to a specific constituent or project. These personal files should be coded using the appropriate position number. These are your personal files and are designed to be helpful to you and those who follow you. Please see the assistant to the associate vice president for your position number.
3. **Project files:** These contain documents that are not related to a specific constituent. These are specific items that pertain to the planning and outcome of events.

Project files and documents will be coded using a standardized number assigned to every area within the university. Each individual area is responsible for determining the use of the range of the numbers allotted. Each individual area is also responsible for creating a standardized method for the coding of the other fields in the document information window. These include, but are not limited to:

CID: This field will be used for the standardized number assigned to the project.

LastName/Org: The last name, organization title, or project name.

Title: A description of the document. Specific projects will have specific document titles, so consult the appendix of the appropriate area when coding.

Doc Date: This is the date the document was created.

Use, if any, of the keys field: These can be used for document summaries, cross-referencing, soft credit, etc.

The assignment of numbers is as follows:

• Alumni Relations	10000-10999	• Athletics	11000-11999
• Annual Fund	20000-20999	• Cox School	41000-41999
• Assoc. VP/Exec. Dir.	60000-60999	• Dedman	21000-21999
• Capital Projects	30000-30999	• Law School	61000-61999
• Corporate/Fdn Relations	40000-40999	• Meadows	31000-31999
• Information Services	50000-50999	• Perkins Theology	71000-71999
• Major Gifts	70000-70999	• SEAS	51000-51999
• Planned Giving	80000-80999	• C U L	95000-95999
• Prospect Research	90000-90999		
• Public Affairs	81000-81999		
• Stewardship	91000-91999		
• Vice President Office	94000-94999		

Each area will break down its range of numbers and assign them to specific projects. The area will also determine the coding of the specific fields of the project files. The project assignments will be added to the policy as they are determined. Additions to the policy will be made in the form of an appendix.

Administrator responsible: Manager, Constituent Records and Data Reporting

March 1, 1995

Chapter 17

Managing Technological Change

■ By Linda Bennett
Executive Director, Development Information Services
Syracuse University

E-mail. Voicemail. Fax machines. Hand-held computers. Client/server technology. The World Wide Web. Internet surfing. Personal home pages. Cell phones. Caller ID. Predictive dialing. DVD cameras.

AAAGGGHHH!

Who can keep up with all of today's information technologies? And there's no indication that things will slow down anytime soon. In fact, I think we're only just beginning to see the assimilation of the so-called Information Age, at home and in the office. Technology has caused us to change the ways we communicate with each other, teach our children, entertain ourselves, and conduct our everyday activities, from banking to shopping.

What does this mean for you in institutional advancement? You can't help noticing that technology has a dramatic impact on how you work. Nowhere is this more evident than in advancement services. If you've been working in the information-services side of development for more than 10 years, you can undoubtedly remember when typewriters abounded, fax machines were scarce, and personal computers were primarily the bailiwick of the "computer people."

But now the tools have changed substantially, including the ones you use to process and record gift and pledge information, update biographical data, deliver lists and reports, perform prospect research, and track major prospects and donors. Your role in providing these tools, and in training your colleagues and information-services staff to use them, has expanded as well. Advancement services is moving rapidly from back-office functions to mission-critical information providers.

As a leader in learning and applying new information technologies, you must understand the impact of change on your staff, your organization, and yourself. The following is a brief introduction to managing technology-enabled change, including what change management is and what techniques you can use to initiate, create, manage, and sustain change successfully.

UNDERSTANDING CHANGE MANAGEMENT AND WHY IT MATTERS

Change management can be defined in two ways: first, as a process of helping people make major alterations in their work environment; and second, as a set of techniques to create and sustain change within an organization. Being able to sustain change is by no means a given, nor is it easy.

Change management is important because it's so critical to achieving the vision of your organization or department. "Vision" describes the future state or where you want to be after changes have been implemented. But before you can achieve that vision, you must do several things that are all a part of change management:

1. **Understand what has caused the need for change.** Possibilities include external mandates, new management, new business processes, and new equipment or technology. Understanding what drives change helps you build the case and consensus for change and define its scope.

2. **Determine whether change is being driven from the top down or the bottom up, and who supports the change politically and financially.** When technology drives change, top-down support is essential for many reasons, including political consid-

erations, morale, and money. As far as money is concerned, higher-ups need to be in favor because funds for training, technology infrastructures, and upgraded software or hardware must be viewed as annual budget items rather than one-time capital costs.

3. **Define the vision.** Perhaps you want a paperless office, speedier information delivery, or more end-user reporting at the desktop. Define and communicate your future state—your vision—and then map out the path, define your goals, and chart the milestones to get there.

> *Change management is important because it's so critical to achieving the vision of your organization or department.*

4. **Identify and involve stakeholders, the people and departments most affected by the change.** For example, when you implement a new information system, you're sure to influence the business processes in the annual fund, donor relations, and major gifts offices as well as in advancement services. But they're not the only ones. The programming staff will feel the impact because its reporting tools and programming languages will be altered. And the central information systems and systems support staff will change with the coming of new computing platforms, operating systems, or hardware.

The implication is clear: Early on, you must involve all stakeholders in the change process. They need to understand what is happening and why; have input into the process; and work with you to implement the change successfully rather than resist the new technology and changes it causes.

5. **Recognize the barriers to change.** Why would stakeholders resist? Because your organizational culture may not be in tune with the need for change. You may well be up against many barriers, including staff who are unready or unwilling to change, afraid or threatened by change, and actively working against it.

This is where change management comes in. To reduce the barriers, you need to plan for change and build consensus, develop and communicate your plan, train and re-train staff as needed, communicate your progress, and measure your results.

PLANNING FOR CHANGE

A plan is important for several reasons. For one thing, it helps you recognize and control the impact of change on the social and organizational fabric of your office. Recognizing the social impact is critical because, as we've already noted, human attitudes can effectively block change from happening. To prevent this, all involved need to understand what's happening and when, and how they and their jobs will be affected.

For another thing, a plan helps you prepare people to apply technologies in new ways or different jobs, and forces you to review, revise, and document the flow of work and the processes involved. You need to make sure both that the technology can support any new processes you plan (or are forced to incorporate) and that it can be integrated into the technologies already in place.

Planning and managing such technology-enabled change also requires a dedicated team of people with diverse backgrounds and technical and business expertise. You need to identify the leaders and managers who buy in to the change-management project and who can make decisions, manage tasks, measure progress, and create alternatives to planned initiatives when necessary. Such people are vital to your project's success. From among this group of people, you select key players to work on incorporating your plan for change into your project plan. As you go along, you also need to gain consensus and approval from management as the team develops the project plans.

Once it's time to develop your plan, be sure to follow these important steps:

- **Assess the readiness to change and to commit to your specific goal.** Will your current institutional culture help or hinder the process? Determine how to progress under each scenario using "if, then" or "best case/worst case" analysis, which will help you think about contingency plans ahead of time.
- **Identify who will be the change agents and leaders of change** and be aware that these people may and should come from different levels of the institution.
- **Decide where specific changes will occur and who will be affected.** People will react better if they understand what specific processes will change and why, and how the changes will affect them. Keeping them in the know and providing training will help greatly to ease the transition from your old technology and work processes to new ones.
- **Communicate, communicate, communicate.** Before you

> *The learning curve for new systems and technology is usually steeper than you'd imagine.*

MANAGING TECHNOLOGICAL CHANGE

start to implement your overall plan, devise a communications plan to sell the change to all stakeholders and to inform others who are less affected by the change. It's critical to educate staff at the grassroots level. Acknowledge the fear, resistance, and uncertainty change brings on. But remain determined to press on to achieve your goal.

Inevitably, staff will experience frustration, chaos, and turmoil—and that's when they know what to expect! So share your plan and communicate the benefits of change often and clearly. Communicating your vision for the future enables you as a manager to help your staff and colleagues succeed in making major changes in how they can and will perform their work. Of equal importance, it contributes to a better understanding of how work processes will change and improve, which in turn helps break down fear of and resistance to change. Knowing what's going to happen, and how and when, greatly reduces the apprehension that change can cause.

TRAINING AND RE-TRAINING STAFF

When new technology drives change, you become fully aware of technology's impact on your job, your workflow, your productivity, and your stress level. This knowledge also helps you to predict the likely reaction to changes being made.

For example, in implementing a new information system, you know at least in the abstract that a new system will bring about disruptions in your work processes and flow. What you may not be able to fully grasp is the scope of the change. Tasks that were familiar to you, and even rote, have to be relearned, reworked, or eliminated altogether and replaced with new processes. Many of your established routines disappear or cease being routine. Some skill sets are no longer applicable, valued, or considered laudatory. This is difficult for people who for years have been rewarded for a particular skill that new technology makes obsolete.

The learning curve for new systems and technology is usually steeper than you'd imagine. More sophisticated systems, software, and retrieval tools can take a long time to figure out and require continuous attention as vendors and software developers make upgrades and fix bugs.

Training and re-training become critical success factors; again, that's why management must see them as base-budget or line-item necessities, not areas to cut when budgets tighten. People need to stay current on new software, new processes, and new procedures. Many of your procedures and frames of reference will change due to the new technology, and many of your policies will need to be revised to take advantage of the functionality new technology offers. Training is essential to getting change accomplished well.

In fact, this is a good time to point out that the only constant you can count on is your knowledge of the fundamental business of development. That will not change just because you're acquiring new tools, new skills, and greater expertise. Still, you must work diligently to avoid the trap of concentrating so heavily on making the technology work that you neglect the business side of the equation in the process.

> *Training and re-training become critical success factors; again, that's why management must see them as base-budget or line-item necessities, not areas to cut when budgets tighten.*

COMMUNICATING PROGRESS

Just as it's impossible to over-communicate your plan, it's impossible to over-communicate your progress. People want and need to know what's going on. Be honest even if you fail to meet deadlines and milestones. Let your constituency know what is happening and why.

As part of this, remember that audiences vary widely, and so should the communication formats you use. Certain people only pay attention to formal memos or paper newsletters; others prefer the Web or e-mail; some senior executives want to hear what's happening rather than read about it. If top management does want a memo, do your best to keep it short.

MEASURING YOUR RESULTS

How do you know if you've achieved your plan's goals and reached the future state you envisioned? Without a benchmark to measure your results, it will be difficult to tell. Setting benchmarks is part of change management. Ask such questions as, can people use the technology? Are they able to generate the reports they need? Can they store the data they want? Do they understand the meaning of the information they're getting? Then measure your answers against your expectations.

Be sure the technology is not an end in itself but rather a useful tool for everyone in institutional advancement. Work to ensure that the technology supports your business and its implementation, and that its use is driven by business needs.

CELEBRATING YOUR SUCCESS

Finally, when your department has met its last deadline and your project is complete, celebrate your team's successes. Give credit to all who were involved in the project. Look back, see how far you've come, and take the time to appreciate what you've accomplished. The next project will come all too soon.

References

Bond, Victor. *"Change Management."* La Jolla, CA: ChangeNet: The Business Transformation Group, 1994.

Galpin, Timothy J. *The Human Side of Change.* San Francisco: Jossey-Bass, 1996.

Price Waterhouse Change Integration Team. *Better Change: Best Practices for Transforming Your Organization.* Chicago: Irwin Professional Publishing, 1995.

Schein, E. *Organizational Change and Leadership.* San Francisco: Jossey-Bass, 1992. Schneider, Polly, Finding the Right Chemistry, CIO Magazine, November 1, 1998, pp. 37-44.

Personal interviews with Professors Robert Benjamin and Steve Sawyer, School of Information Studies, Syracuse University, 1996-1998.

Section V

Management

Creating Comparative Reports: Three Ways to Track Progress in Your Fund-raising Performance

■ By Madelyn Miller
Director, Development Services
Case Western Reserve University

As an old adage goes, "You can't figure out where you're going until you see where you've been." That's why you and the rest of your advancement services staff should gather data, analyze them, and then prepare reports that give insights into both your institution's fund-raising performance and that of your peer campuses. Such comparative reports are valuable in two major ways. They help with strategic planning by uncovering your development office's strengths and weaknesses, and they form a statistical basis for setting private-support priorities and goals.

"Comparative reports were part of the fabric of the strategy we developed for fund raising in the new millennium," says Bruce A. Loessin, vice president for development and alumni affairs at my institution, Case Western Reserve University. "They provided the context by which we judged areas of opportunities and national trends in philanthropy."

Although your office can use comparative reports to make your institution look good, at times they may uncover findings that make it look not so good. Don't worry. You still haven't wasted your time. Reports that reveal weakness can show internal staff the areas that need more attention and help convince your administration to invest in areas that need shoring up.

There are three basic categories of comparative private-support reporting:

1. Institutional internal reporting typically shows your institution's historical data on private support by source, by fund account, and by the schools or management centers within your campus. These reports highlight giving trends and the impact of your past fund-raising efforts.

2. National ranking reporting compares data from your institution with data from other educational institutions nationally. These reports can display comparison data from all national institutions or from subsets of institutions categorized by the Carnegie Classification of Institutions of Higher Education.

3. Peer group reporting displays data for 10 to 12 institutions that are similar in nature to your own. You determine your peer group by examining similarities in, among other things, student enrollment, size of alumni base, and size of endowment.

For purposes of this chapter, we will assume that, every month, your advancement services office already prepares at least a cumulative private support report by source, fund account, and school, if your institution has more than one management center. We'll also assume you use the CASE Management Reporting Standards as the basis for recording private support data in your database. The need for reports is one of the best reasons for adhering to the CASE standards. They provide universal definitions for what constitutes an alumnus and what can be considered unrestricted giving, to name just two topics. When you use the standards and analyze data from peer institutions that do likewise, you can feel confident that you're comparing apples to apples and getting reliable results.

Let's examine the subject of reports in two parts. First we'll look at the basic steps to gathering and organizing your data.

Then we'll discuss the best ways to handle each of the three most important types of reports.

REPORTING BASICS

Getting started

Before you begin to create a set of comparative reports, identify both their purpose and the audience you're targeting. These will drive the types of reports you create—and the results they bring your development office.

Here are two examples from Case Western Reserve University. Our collection process dates back to 1985, when we first used it to measure our performance against that of other private research institutions as a means to educate higher-ups about the realities of fund raising. Those early findings helped convince our president and trustees that although we were spending only 3 cents to raise a dollar, we were raising much less than our peers and needed to invest more.

Another major use was to show both internal and external decision makers who our fund-raising "competition" was and to set our sights according to our national peers, not smaller not-for-profits in our home town. Recalls Susan Stevens Jaros, associate vice president for development and alumni affairs, "This wasn't really to compete for dollars with other private research institutions but rather to say that Case Western Reserve University should be doing in Cleveland what Duke is doing in Raleigh-Durham and Johns Hopkins is doing in Baltimore."

Gathering your data

One of the most important decisions you must make before you begin your research is how to define your data source or sources.

For internal data comparisons, you must decide whether to extract your data from historical hard copy reports or to pull data from your computer system. If you use reports that were produced historically, you'll be reporting data as they were recorded in the year in which the report was produced. Obviously, this is the optimum choice.

However, the downside to using historical-report documents is that you may not have the data in the format you need if the information was not classified then as it is today. If this is the case, you have no choice but to use the data in your computer system, providing your institution has stored historical data in its database.

There is also a downside to doing extracts of historical data from your computer system. Over time, there may have been changes to the data in your database, such as to entity record types, source codes, pledge status codes, and so on. These data changes may affect the information so that when it is totaled, it does not match the final reported totals of any given year. If this happens, you need to footnote any data discrepancies.

You can choose to use a mix of historical reports and computer extracts to acquire the data needed, but again, you need to remember to note any data deviations that appear. And always indicate your data source or sources on the bottom of the report so that you know the origin of the information.

For national and peer group comparisons, the Council for Aid to Education's *Voluntary Support of Education* survey is the best source of data for both your institution and, obviously, other institutions. The VSE survey provides extensive information for comparative analysis, such as total private support data, data by source, capital and current operations totals, information on planned gifts, corporate matching gift data, statistics on E & G (Education and General) expenditures, endowment market value, and enrollment.

If you have access to the World Wide Web, VSE Data Miner is an outstanding tool to use when gathering data about other institutions. Among other things, it lets you access 10 years of VSE survey data for most educational institutions. Many of Data Miner's features make data gathering fast and efficient; it's even easy to create charts and graphs. Available by annual subscription from CAE, it's well worth the annual subscription fee if you plan to do regular comparison reporting.

Choosing the best report format for you

Comparison reports can be as simple as a list sorted high to low or as complex as a multi-level graph. For example, if you simply want to display alumni giving trends, a list of 10 or 15 years of total alumni giving may suffice, or you may want to create a graph using software such as Harvard Graphics.

But you can also do more complex reports that compare averages over a certain number of years or that display pre-campaign giving, giving during a campaign, and post-campaign giving. Again, keep in mind the point of your analysis and the audience for whom the report is intended. These two factors will drive how simple or how complex your report format should be.

HANDLING SPECIFIC TYPES OF REPORTS

1. Internal comparative reporting

Internal comparative reports are used to get a historical perspective on your institution, to identify its strengths and weaknesses, and to track your institutional philanthropic trends. Internal comparative statistics are helpful if your institution is doing strategic planning or contemplating a capital campaign. The following are examples of some standard internal comparative report formats.

- **Historical analysis of private support totals.** These data show whether your institution is continuing to increase private support annually. A simple graph produced in Harvard Graphics with time on the X-axis and dollars on the Y-axis is an excellent format to use to display this data.

  You can also add a trend line to plot private support trends (see Figure 18-1).

- **Historical analysis of private support by school within your institution.** Just like the historical analysis of private support report, this is best done in a Harvard Graphics chart with time on the X-axis and dollars on the Y-axis. Another way to display the data is with a simple chart called the box chart (Figure 18-2). This format easily shows which of your schools is raising dollars. You can present the chart with or without a box drawn around a particular school on which you want to focus attention.

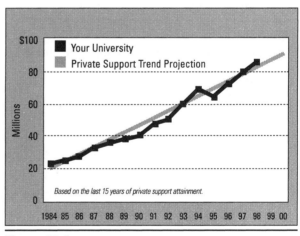

Figure 18-1
Historical Analysis of Private Support Totals

- **Historical analysis of private support by source.** This report gives perspective by such VSE survey sources as

FISCAL YEAR	1	2	3	4	5	6	7	8	9	10
1985	Engineering $10,452,775	Medicine $9,338,641	Agriculture $3,060,734	Arts & Sci. $2,253,863	Education $1,642,373	Law $1,372,263	Management $1,226,809	Social Work $854,735	Nursing $626,926	Dentistry $413,661
1986	Engineering $7,041,652	Medicine $6,983,622	Agriculture $2,552,868	Management $2,292,392	Arts & Sci. $2,091,783	Law $1,686,978	Education $1,538,888	Social Work $1,279,084	Nursing $698,559	Dentistry $239,609
1987	Medicine $9,770,168	Engineering $7,239,842	Education $4,018,645	Agriculture $3,925,476	Management $2,698,939	Arts & Sci. $2,071,152	Social Work $1,738,253	Nursing $1,167,976	Law $1,097,689	Dentistry $278,794
1988	Engineering $9,498,681	Medicine $9,069,309	Education $3,567,508	Agriculture $2,915,734	Management $2,883,345	Arts & Sci. $2,536,423	Law $1,179,712	Nursing $1,067,448	Social Work $999,181	Dentistry $342,016
1989	Medicine $9,404,035	Engineering $7,072,419	Agriculture $6,008,239	Arts & Sci. $2,905,687	Management $2,645,869	Social Work $1,945,763	Education $1,750,848	Law $1,605,138	Nursing $1,161,694	Dentistry $476,392
1990	Medicine $11,138,714	Engineering $9,448,572	Arts & Sci. $4,924,833	Agriculture $4,431,417	Management $3,105,730	Law $2,160,569	Social Work $2,139,359	Nursing $1,512,592	Education $1,432,335	Dentistry $466,036
1991	Medicine $12,377,215	Agriculture $9,467,628	Management $6,243,267	Engineering $5,339,475	Law $4,924,252	Arts & Sci. $3,780,565	Nursing $2,599,806	Social Work $2,280,993	Education $2,208,041	Dentistry $538,722
1992	Medicine $14,009,334	Agriculture $10,824,420	Arts & Sci. $6,382,904	Management $6,044,882	Engineering $5,746,569	Law $4,573,623	Nursing $4,074,895	Education $3,755,319	Social Work $2,452,881	Dentistry $578,086
1993	Medicine $13,967,025	Engineering $11,762,212	Agriculture $8,840,319	Arts & Sci. $7,746,274	Nursing $5,670,857	Management $4,222,956	Law $3,362,972	Education $2,580,071	Social Work $2,086,426	Dentistry $711,538
1994	Medicine $18,074,037	Agriculture $15,401,150	Engineering $11,371,105	Law $7,925,285	Arts & Sci. $6,143,904	Nursing $5,450,300	Management $5,249,352	Education $4,048,426	Social Work $2,839,093	Dentistry $500,224
1995	Medicine $16,524,422	Engineering $11,482,515	Agriculture $10,306,719	Management $5,717,541	Arts & Sci. $5,589,947	Nursing $3,630,425	Law $3,492,007	Education $3,321,775	Social Work $2,268,329	Dentistry $406,638
1996	Medicine $18,803,475	Engineering $18,185,545	Agriculture $9,841,264	Arts & Sci. $8,382,253	Nursing $5,051,733	Management $4,436,871	Education $4,385,163	Law $2,554,271	Social Work $2,473,341	Dentistry $1,021,340
1997	Medicine $21,056,447	Engineering $13,393,132	Management $11,085,672	Agriculture $9,680,820	Engineering $8,181,819	Education $4,079,647	Nursing $2,681,421	Social Work $2,283,643	Law $2,081,690	Dentistry $751,884
1998	Medicine $29,205,089	Arts & Sci. $15,308,642	Agriculture $9,769,014	Engineering $8,434,938	Management $7,833,248	Nursing $6,021,161	Social Work $3,720,455	Education $2,804,590	Law $2,507,117	Dentistry $901,271

Source: Historical Fiscal Year Reports

Figure 18-2
Your University Management Center Comparison
Private Support Attainment by Fiscal Year: 1985-1998

alumni, corporations and corporate foundations, foundations and family foundations, associations, friends, parents, and trustees. You can easily graph these data or put them in a box chart (Figure 18-3). You can also use this kind of format for a historical analysis of private support by source for each school within your institution.

• **Historical report of private support by fund account.** This report gives historical perspective by endowment, current support, and capital dollars. These data are also easy to graph to show trends over time.

In addition to these four, two other types of historical comparative reports are useful. One is a report that graphs cost per dollars raised. By comparing your development budget to private support dollars raised, you'll be able to track fund-raising effectiveness.

SOURCE	RANK BY PRIVATE SUPPORT								
	1	2	3	4	5	6	7	8	9
ALUMNI	Arts & Sci. $6,460,638	Medicine $5,320,097	Nursing $5,306,752	Engineering $3,683,092	Agriculture $3,056,126	Law $1,494,376	Social Work $1,375,842	Dentistry $420,299	Management $236,770
% of Private Support	42.20%	18.22%	88.14%	43.66%	31.28%	59.61%	36.98%	46.63%	3.02%
CORPORATE	Medicine $2,582,802	Engineering $1,434,124	Management $1,379,294	Agriculture $739,617	Arts & Sci. $389,722	Law $214,558	Dentistry $136,282	Nursing $30,628	Social Work $12,728
% of Private Support	8.84%	17.00%	17.61%	7.57%	2.55%	8.56%	15.12%	0.51%	0.34%
FOUNDATION	Medicine $9,630,242	Arts & Sci. $5,515,056	Agriculture $2,877,238	Management $2,492,820	Social Work $2,125,684	Engineering $1,647,501	Nursing $342,983	Law $321,627	Dentistry $164,227
% of Private Support	32.97%	36.03%	29.45%	31.82%	57.14%	19.53%	5.70%	12.83%	18.22%
TRUSTEE	Arts & Sci. $1,438,233	Agriculture $663,631	Medicine $629,513	Engineering $271,407	Management $21,275	Nursing $9,572	Law $5,800	Social Work $750	Dentistry $0
% of Private Support	9.39%	6.79%	2.16%	3.22%	0.27%	0.16%	0.23%	0.02%	0.00%
FACULTY/STAFF	Medicine $512,749	Engineering $178,302	Arts & Sci. $138,153	Dentistry $134,679	Social Work $89,923	Nursing $82,311	Agriculture $51,171	Law $10,148	Management $7,380
% of Private Support	1.76%	2.11%	0.90%	14.94%	2.42%	1.37%	0.52%	0.40%	0.09%
FRIENDS	Management $3,657,108	Medicine $3,316,806	Agriculture $2,094,122	Engineering $1,002,193	Arts & Sci. $453,898	Law $410,690	Nursing $213,630	Dentistry $31,482	Social Work $3,825
% of Private Support	46.69%	11.36%	21.44%	11.88%	2.96%	16.38%	3.55%	3.49%	0.10%
PARENTS	Engineering $12,002	Arts & Sci. $11,140	Agriculture $8,850	Medicine $3,315	Nursing $1,447	Law $150	Dentistry $100	Management $50	Social Work $0
% of Private Support	0.14%	0.07%	0.09%	0.01%	0.02%	0.01%	0.01%	0.00%	0.00%
ASSOCIATIONS	Medicine $7,209,566	Arts & Sci. $901,802	Agriculture $278,259	Engineering $206,317	Social Work $111,703	Law $49,769	Management $38,550	Nursing $33,838	Dentistry $14,202
% of Private Support	24.69%	5.89%	2.85%	2.45%	3.00%	1.99%	0.49%	0.56%	1.58%
PRIVATE SUPPORT	Medicine $29,205,089	Arts & Sci. $15,308,642	Agriculture $9,769,014	Engineering* $8,434,938	Management $7,833,248	Nursing $6,021,161	Social Work $3,720,455	Law $2,507,117	Dentistry $901,271

Source: 1998 Fiscal Year Private Support Report

Figure 18-3
Your University Management Center Comparison
Private Support Attainment by Source: Fiscal Year 1998
Source Attainment as a Percent of Private Support

Another is an analysis and comparison during pre-campaign, campaign, and post-campaign years. One way to format these data is to graph your private support attainment during these three periods of time, calculate your averages, and display them on the graph (Figure 18-4). Again, this type of report is invaluable for strategic or campaign planning because it tracks fundraising performance over a significant period of time.

2. National ranking reports

These reports are important for measuring your institution's fund-raising performance against that of other national institutions. One of the most basic formats is simply a comparative list of the top 25 or 50 institutions in the country ranked high to low by total private support. To provide a gauge to measure trends, your report should also include the same ranking for the previ-

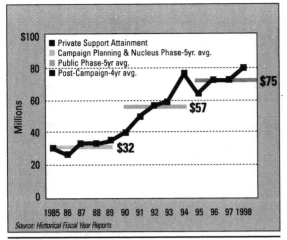

Figure 18-4

Your University Private Support Analysis

Fiscal Year Private Support Attainment: 1985-1998

ous fiscal year. This format makes it easy to see the movement in rank among the institutions (Figure 18-5).

A set of reports that compares your institution with others at the national level should also include comparisons for your Carnegie Classification of Institutions of Higher Education Group. This subset is often more relevant and interesting to compare because the institutions are similar; if you're a major private research university, you're naturally more interested in comparing yourself to other private research universities. You should prepare comparative reports for total private support rank for your Carnegie classification group as well as by source and fund account.

It's useful as well to analyze comparative data for your Carnegie classification group over time. It's simple to do a two-

INSTITUTION	FY96 RANK	FY96 TPS	INSTITUTION	FY97 RANK	FY97 TPS
Stanford University	1	312.8	Harvard University	1	427.6
Harvard University	2	309.3	Stanford University	2	312.2
Cornell University	3	219.7	Cornell University	3	220.6
Duke University	4	181.2	Duke University	4	219.9
Yale University	5	172.1	Yale University	5	203.1
Columbia University	6	163.8	Columbia University	6	201.7
University of Pennsylvania	7	153.1	University of Pennsylvania	7	174.5
Massachusetts Institute of Technology	8	132.4	Johns Hopkins University	8	164.5
University of Southern California	9	128.5	University of Southern California	9	154.1
University of Chicago	10	126.9	Massachusetts Institute of Technology	10	137.3
Johns Hopkins University	11	125.8	Princeton University	11	133.8
Princeton University	12	117.3	University of Chicago	12	129.1
Northwestern University	13	107.8	Northwestern University	13	124.6
New York University	14	90.9	New York University	14	109.8
Dartmouth College	15	90.9	Washington University	15	92.7
Washington University	16	84.4	Carnegie Mellon	16	90.0
Pepperdine University	17	79.6	University of Miami	17	78.2
University of Notre Dame	18	75.6	Vanderbilt University	18	78.0
Case Western Reserve University	19	75.1	Georgetown University	19	76.6
Brown University	20	72.1	Case Western Reserve University	20	75.2
University of Miami	21	70.9	Brown University	21	67.4
Vanderbilt University	22	62.2	California Institute of Technology	22	67.1
California Institute of Technology	23	62.1	Boston University	23	50.2
Georgetown University	24	53.9	Tufts University	24	45.9
William Marsh Rice University	25	50.7	Rockefeller University	25	37.4

Source: 1996 Voluntary Support of Education; 1997 Voluntary Support of Education, Council for Aid to Education

Figure 18-5

Top 25 Private Universities & Colleges—FY 1996 v. FY 1997—Total Private Support (in millions)

year comparison by laying out the data side by side on a report. It's also interesting to analyze data over five- or 10-year periods; you can display this comparison with a graph prepared in Harvard Graphics or in a spreadsheet format. Doing a giving analysis over a significant time period will give a true sense of philanthropic trends for your particular group.

Another way to look at comparative giving is to calculate the percent change in giving between two distinct periods of time. To do this, gather 10 years of total private support data for your Carnegie classification group. Compare the average total private support for the first five years of giving with the average total private support for the second five years. Then calculate the percent change between the two averages. Once you have your percent change data, you can rank the institutions high to low based upon these numbers (Figure 18-6). This type of comparative analysis works for data by source and fund account as well. When calculating your averages, you may want to eliminate the high and low figures for each school to guard against averaging in high one-time gifts or windfalls.

Using average-percent-change data for institutional comparisons is an excellent way to show off your institution's strengths. Let's say your institution ranks 30th in the country in total private support, but you know you've been particularly strong in raising dollars for buildings over the past decade. When you calculate your average percent change over the past 10 years and compare it with that of others in the buildings category, you could rank No. 1 nationally.

Another useful way to analyze fund-raising performance among your Carnegie classification group is to do comparisons based upon total private support by student. This analysis is helpful when you're comparing large institutions with smaller

SOURCE: BUILDINGS

SCHOOL	% AVERAGE CHANGE 85-90 V. 91-96
Your University	463.69%
University A	201.53%
University B	120.55%
University C	102.03%
University D	96.14%
University E	90.98%
University F	66.89%
University G	57.72%
University H	43.78%
University I	40.24%
University J	39.49%
University K	34.42%
Univeristy L	34.04%
University M	26.64%
University N	23.48%
University O	22.75%
University P	19.14%
University Q	16.81%
University R	14.72%
University S	13.42%
University T	11.33%
University U	11.27%
University V	-7.87%
University W	-15.32%
University X	-16.77%
University Y	-21.40%
University Z	-23.86%
University AA	-24.40%
University BB	-30.40%
University CC	-45.25%
University DD	-49.46%
University EE	-50.06%
University FF	-51.94%
University GG	-64.29%
MEAN AVERAGE CHANGE:	**33.83%**

Source: CAE Data Miner

Figure 18-6
Analysis of 34 Private Research Universities

FY	1	2	3	4	5	6	7	8	9	10
1986	University A $22,609,720	University B $21,677,780	University C $14,084,230	University D $13,636,090	University E $13,342,450	University F $12,729,030	University G $10,394,710	University H $8,046,002	University I $7,456,737	University J $3,128,323
1987	University A $29,199,560	University D $29,183,230	University C $20,358,130	University E $17,858,270	University G $13,174,510	University F $13,168,910	University H $12,124,240	University B $9,342,987	University J $8,342,417	University I $7,609,424
1988	University C $23,867,910	University A $18,654,420	University D $15,676,680	University E $14,712,570	University G $12,995,970	University F $12,889,600	University H $10,541,130	University B $8,845,171	University I $8,137,067	University J $8,041,653
1989	University A $24,828,240	University F $19,635,080	University D $18,733,760	University C $18,296,500	University G $17,717,990	University E $15,464,090	University H $10,968,330	University B $8,821,352	University I $8,214,755	University J $5,758,360
1990	University F $31,668,280	University A $24,392,520	University D $22,670,580	University G $21,536,850	University C $16,331,200	University E $12,983,150	University B $12,921,400	University H $9,182,495	University I $8,236,059	University J $8,155,695
1991	University D $28,959,750	University A $25,941,620	University F $21,099,890	University E $18,196,570	University C $17,346,020	University G $17,197,100	University B $13,086,800	University H $11,473,100	University I $9,659,709	University J $9,545,524
1992	University A $39,518,410	University C $28,551,090	University E $21,286,090	University B $19,528,000	University G $18,634,430	University F $17,632,690	University H $17,191,420	University D $14,531,490	University J $14,483,530	University I $12,735,640
1993	University A $33,727,243	University E $22,409,529	University J $21,923,911	University G $21,025,594	University C $20,029,083	University F $17,889,148	University D $16,179,780	University H $15,078,033	University I $14,723,193	University B $12,312,512
1994	University A $45,066,766	University C $25,493,738	University H $25,192,353	University D $21,117,760	University F $19,006,395	University G $18,495,342	University B $18,172,030	University E $16,435,966	University I $16,130,712	University J $8,489,582
1995	University A $41,653,345	University D $35,602,287	University C $27,560,972	University F $24,581,997	University J $24,162,524	University E. $23,109,014	University G $22,739,914	University H $17,871,083	University B $16,546,229	University I $15,456,725
1996	University A $50,876,896	University G $33,239,549	University D $29,613,614	University E $28,004,338	University C $27,859,394	University F $22,859,759	University H $16,874,193	University B $14,148,670	University I $12,841,610	University J $11,430,934
1997	University C $52,293,483	University F $49,382,259	University A $46,663,860	University E $39,928,622	University G $37,011,376	University B $22,882,456	University D $22,568,512	University H $19,435,636	University I $13,121,987	University I $12,879,653

Source: CAE Data Miner

Figure 18-7

Your University Peer Group Giving—Alumni/ae Comparsion: Based on 1986-97 Fiscal Private Support

institutions because it puts the dollars raised into perspective based on institutional size.

3. Peer group reporting

Whittling your Carnegie classification group down to peer groups allows you to make more extensive and more relevant comparisons. For one thing, your comparison group is smaller and easier to manage; for another, the data for the institutions to which you're comparing yourself are significantly more pertinent because you're comparing like institutions. Peer group comparisons are particularly helpful when you're measuring fund-raising performance and trends. These reports can show strengths and weaknesses within your institution as well as educate internal constituencies about your advancement team's goals and priorities.

When compiling your peer group, consider, among other things, size of endowment, size of enrollment, number of alumni, or structure of the institution. Ten or 12 institutions are usually enough to provide relevant comparisons.

Once you've identified your peers, any and all of the reports we've discussed previously would work well. It's easy to show total private support by peer group, again either in a format like box charts or by graphing total private support using Harvard Graphics (Figure 18-7). Ten to 12 years of comparative data for each institution will give you a sense of the trends. Be sure to include private support by source and by fund account in your reports as well.

So there you have it: the many reasons why gathering, analyzing, and presenting data in comparative reports is an important job for your advancement services office. If you've never done such reports before, starting now will be a great benefit for years to come. After all, reports that make your institution look good can make you look good as well.

References

CASE. *CASE Management Reporting Standards: Standards for Annual Giving and Campaigns in Educational Fund Raising.* Washington, DC: CASE, 1996.

CASE. *CASE Report of Educational Fund-Raising Campaigns 1994-95.* Washington, DC: CASE, 1996.

CASE. *Fund-Raising Standards for Annual Giving and Campaign Reports: For Not-For-Profit Organizations Other Than Colleges and Universities, and Schools.* Washington, DC: CASE, 1998.

Morgan, David R. *Voluntary Support of Education.* New York, NY: Council for Aid to Education. Co-sponsored by CASE and the National Association of Independent Schools. Published annually.

Mercer, Joye. "Fund Raisers Differ on the Value of Statistics Showing the Percentage of Alumni Who Give: While Some Point to Figures With Pride, Others Say That Some Colleges Manipulate the Data," *Chronicle of Higher Education* 44, no. 27 (July 12, 1996): A33-A34.

Stehle, Vince. "Study Finds Variations in How Campaign Gifts are Reported," *Chronicle of Philanthropy* 9, no. 6 (January 9, 1997): 27.

Taylor, John H. "The New Marching Orders: Revised Reporting Standards for Annual Giving Take Effect the July. Here's a Quick Guide for Those in the Trenches," CURRENTS 23, no. 2 (February 1997): 36-37.

Chapter 19

Improving Office Communication: How Understanding Different Learning Styles Helps Get Your Message Across

■ By Vicky Medlock
Assistant Vice President for Advancement Services
University of South Florida

Few things are as frustrating as the inability to communicate. This frustration is greatly exacerbated in the office, where co-workers sometimes seem incapable of speaking so that they can understand each other.

If a statement seems clear as it leaves your mouth but it's received as near-gibberish by your colleagues, chances are they simply don't digest information the same way you do. That's why the technique that works when you talk to your shy, sensitive colleague in the next cubicle might not get you ahead with your extroverted, decisive boss. Knowing their individual learning styles can help you tailor your style of communication so they actually receive your message.

OK, so I'm introducing a new term: "learning styles." In an article, authors Clay Johnston and Carol J. Orwig define learning styles as "… a collection of individual skills and preferences that affect how a person perceives, gathers, and processes information." Words may have the power to move entire nations, but they're meaningless if they're not understood. That's why we must explore the wide, wonderful world of learning styles. Start by taking the following quick test to determine your own strongest learning style.

1. If I have business to conduct or a need to interact with another person, I prefer:
   A. A face-to-face meeting.
   B. The telephone, since it saves time.
   C. Talking while walking, jogging, or doing something physical and taking advantage of all free time.

2. At a meeting I:
   A. Come prepared with notes and displays.
   B. Enjoy discussing issues and hearing others' points of view.
   C. Would rather be somewhere else and so spend my time doodling.

3. The most effective way to reward someone is:
   A. A written note of thanks.
   B. Spoken praise to the person or a group.
   C. A pat on the back.

4. When I'm angry, I usually:
   A. Clam up and give others the silent treatment.
   B. Am quick to let others know why I'm angry.
   C. Clench my fists, grasp something tightly, or storm off.

5. When working on a donor proposal presentation, I generally:
   A. Use lots of charts and photographs with my copy.
   B. Think more about how I will present the proposal than how it will look on paper.
   C. Encourage the prospect to visit campus for a tour.

How did you do? If you answered A to all or most of the questions, you are a visual learner. If you answered B to all or most, you are an auditory learner. If you answered mostly C, you are a kinesthetic/tactual learner. Here are definitions of all three types.

1. **Visual learners** learn by seeing. They like to look around and examine a situation. They think in pictures and details and have vivid imaginations. Neat and meticulous in appearance, they generally come prepared and take copious and detailed notes.

Visual people may be quiet and become impatient when they have to listen extensively. Facial expression is a good index of their emotions; they often stare when angry or beam when happy.

Words may have the power to move entire nations, but they're meaningless if they're not understood.

These types have greater immediate recall of things that are presented visually, which is why they remember faces but forget names. Relatively unaware of sounds, they can be distracted by visual disorder or movement. Finally, visual learners solve problems in a deliberate fashion, making plans and organizing their thoughts by writing them down.

2. **Auditory learners** like to talk through what they're learning. They enjoy listening but can hardly wait for a chance to speak. They tend toward long and repetitive descriptions. They express their feeling by shouting for joy, blowing up verbally, and indicating emotion through the tone, pitch, and volume of their voices.

Auditory types like reading dialogue but dislike lengthy narratives and descriptions. Frequently, they move their lips or speak under their breath while reading. They have good auditory work-attack skills and feel their way through problems by talking about each step or course of action.

Auditory people will often take the lead on group projects; this provides them with additional opportunities to summarize and restate other comments verbally.

3. **Kinesthetic/tactual learners** try things out by touching, feeling, and manipulating. They learn best by doing and remember best what has been done, not what they've seen or talked about. They need direct involvement in what they're learning.

K/T types express their feelings physically—they jump for

joy, push, tug, stomp, and pound. Body tension is a good index of their emotions.

Kinesthetic/tactual people gesture when speaking, are poor listeners, stand close when talking or listening, and quickly lose interest in long verbal discourse. The kinesthetic/tactual learner is rarely comfortable just sitting in a meeting or behind a desk.

DISCERNING OTHER PEOPLE'S STYLES

Now that you have a basic understanding of visual, auditory, and kinesthetic/tactual learners, applying this knowledge to your everyday office life is the next challenge. How do you determine someone else's learning style?

You could have them take the short quiz above and then check their answers. But if that isn't appropriate, use this hypothetical example to see how you'd use your powers of observation to determine learning styles. Let's say you want to approach your boss about a new program that you would like to initiate, but it costs more than $20,000. What's the best way to convince her? Remember these guidelines.

- Again, **visual types** learn best from the written word, looking at pictures or charts, reading from and writing on the board—working with anything they can see. So think about that. Is she inevitably the first to notice a typographical error in your latest publication? Does she often suggest that you send a proposal to her in memo form? If so, she's likely to be a visual learner who would best digest your proposal if you put it in writing with lots of graphs and charts.
- **People with an auditory preference** respond well to lectures, one-to-one meetings, or group discussions. Does your boss like the committee approach to tackling problems? Is she generally not shy about offering a comment or opinion? Then you should present the proposal verbally, giving plenty of opportunities to ask questions,
- **Kinesthetic/tactual colleagues** learn best when they write on paper, get involved with hands-on activities, or take part in small-group activities that enable them to move around or to touch the project at issue. Is your boss an on-the-go person who's out the door visiting with donors much more

than she's in the office? If so, walk her through the proposal with as much hands-on exposure to the idea as possible.

Of course, it would be a mistake to believe that every person fits neatly into one category; in truth, all of us have some visual, auditory, and kinesthetic/tactual traits within us. And there are individuals who have nearly equal strengths in each style. Whatever learning style your co-workers use, the important thing is to understand that it surely does affect how they interpret, solicit, and digest information. The more you tailor your communication accordingly, the more often you and your colleagues will be on the same page.

PUTTING THE PRINCIPLES TO WORK

So that brings up the next question: How, then, can you apply your new-found knowledge to improving general office communication? Here are suggestions for four common situations.

- **Group settings**: Develop presentation techniques that suit varying learning styles. Incorporate all three factors—looking, hearing, and acting—whenever possible. Providing visuals, asking questions, and including an opportunity to move (say, by breaking into smaller groups or writing on the board) will help to stimulate people with each learning style.
- **E-mail**: The visual learner would rather get an e-mail than a phone call. The opposite is true for the auditory person, who may let an e-mail go unanswered for days or weeks. So telephone the auditory type or, better yet, make an appointment to visit face to face. For kinesthetic/tactual learners, e-mail works because it is not passive. Letting their "fingers do the walking" provides at least a modest amount of movement for short-term engagement.
- **Giving instructions**: The visual employee will understand your directions better in writing. The auditory type will prefer verbal instructions. Kinesthetic/tactual learners are always on the go, so go with them. Catch them in the hall and accompany them to their destination as you describe what you want done.
- **Receiving feedback.** For visual learners, written satisfaction surveys work well. But auditory learners would rather that

"Words that convey no information may nevertheless move carloads of shaving cream or cake mix, as we all know from television commercials. Words can start people marching in the streets and can stir others to stoning the marchers. Words that make no sense as prose can make a great deal of sense as poetry. Words that seem simple and clear to some may be puzzling and obscure to others. With words we sugarcoat our nastiest motives and our worst behavior, but with words we also formulate our highest ideals and aspirations."

S. I. Hayakawa, U.S. Senator from California

This quote has stayed with me for nearly two decades, ever since I took an organizational communication class in college. The statement is very true. Words are so important. Who among us hasn't spoken without thinking and ended up with foot in mouth? Who hasn't seen a powerful speaker spur a crowd to action? Who hasn't been moved to tears by the words of a loved one or crushed by the thoughtless words of an acquaintance?

As we turn an eye toward enhancing office communication, it's important to remember Sen. Hayakawa's words and keep foremost in our minds just how powerful words can be.

Still, I would be remiss if I didn't briefly mention nonverbal communication. In no way do I intend to imply that verbal communication is more important. As so many studies of body language have found, nonverbal communication is often as powerful, if not more so, than verbal. (Who doesn't judge a scowling person with crossed arms and legs as less than approachable?)

But for the purposes of this chapter, we'll focus on verbal communication in the office—not just the words we speak but how people learn from what we say and how we choose to say it. Focusing on words and how we present them is crucial to our goal of enhancing communication at work.

you provide opportunities to talk about what would improve their performance. Kinesthetic/tactual learners love the pat on the back for a job well done. They learn best how to improve their performance with a hands-on how-to.

Most important, if you cannot avoid certain activities that don't match up well with a colleague's learning style, look for ways to modify the activities. Even minor adjustments can make a big difference.

In the end, you may wind up using the same words for each kind of person. But once you've adapted your approach, the visual learners around you may find that confusing prose becomes poetry, auditory learners may be inspired to reach for new heights, and the kinesthetic/tactual people may be moved to march in the streets. Matching learning styles to your communication formats will reduce the number of blank stares—and incomplete or incorrect projects—you receive.

In a previous lifetime, I had the opportunity to teach speech communication to a group of college athletes—football players, specifically. Acknowledging their individual learning styles helped me develop activities that took advantage of their natural skills and inclinations. Ultimately, both students and teacher got more out of the experience. You, too, can improve your results by taking a moment to understand your learning style and that of your co-workers. Applying the simple look, hear, and act factors is sure to lead to office communication that's both clearer and more effective.

Postscript to the visual learners: I trust you had no difficulty reading these few pages.

Postscript to the auditory learners: Feel free to have someone read this chapter to you and to comment as you please.

Postscript to the kinesthetic/tactual learners: I recommend reading this chapter as you're walking to your next appointment.

References

Hayakawa, S. I. *Language in Thought and Action,* Fourth Edition. San Francisco, CA: Harcourt Brace Jovanovich Inc. 1978.

Johnston, Clay and Carol J. Orwig. "What Is a Learning Style?" In *Language Learning.* Notes in Linguistics 15 (24-28) 1980.

Barbe, Walter B. and Michael N. Milone, Jr. "Modality," *Instructor,* Vol. 89, No. 6 (January 1980): 44-47.

Swartzman, Joyce. "Learning Styles," *Instructor,* University of South Florida, Tampa, FL, December 1997.

Barron-Tieger, Barbara and Paul Tieger. *The Art of Speedreading People.* Little Brown, 1998.

Chapter 20

Reconciling Advancement Services and Accounting: Five Principles to Help Explain the Relationship and End the Confusion

■ By Jan H. Shimshock
Executive Director, Development
Cranbrook Educational Community

The data report for last month's development activity has just been released. Gifts, grants, and membership in your alumni association and museum are up over the same period of a year ago, with pledges and pledge payments following suit. Across campus, members of the development staff feel justifiably proud of their accomplishments and optimistic about the future.

But then the phone begins to ring and the e-mail starts to appear—as they do every month. Key volunteers and staff are comparing advancement services' recent gift report with the monthly report issued by the accounting department. Board members are curious because your gift and grant totals don't match those on the financial reports. Business and finance staffs are concerned because they can't find a number trail leading to the restricted and unrestricted giving totals. And front-line development colleagues are upset because their records indicate that their annual giving results are being under-reported.

Is advancement services deliberately trying to mislead, or are you and your staff merely inept?

What to do? How can you bridge this gap in knowledge and understanding of gift reporting? Suddenly, as the melody of an old song pops into your head, the answer becomes clearer: "You say potAto, I say potAHto. You say tomAto, I say tomAHto."

The fact is, development services and accounting folks talk about the same things, but we often think and act quite differently. The two groups are like an international team of experts working jointly on a project of mutual benefit. Such projects always have the potential to become an experience straight out of the story of the Tower of Babel. Throw in the fact that your frontline fund raisers frequently have little or no working knowledge of either advancement services or accounting, and the potential for confusion among all parties concerned becomes acute.

To prevent this from happening, and to maintain credibility in the eyes of our constituents (both internal and external), it's important to understand each department's reason for being as well as each other's language. When it comes to reconciling the overlapping activities of advancement services and accounting, there's no substitute for the step-by-step guide, *CASE Management Reporting Standards*, which includes standards for reporting both annual giving and campaign results. As a supplement, however, I offer the following hands-on principles to help you recognize, and then minimize, some key differences between our worlds.

PRINCIPLE NO. 1: WE HAVE DIFFERENT SOURCES OF INDUSTRY STANDARDS.

Development's primary source is the publisher of the book you're reading now, the Council for Advancement and Support of Education. Working with the National Association of College and University Business Officers, CASE periodically issues standards for reporting fund-raising results. The stated purpose of these standards is to guide institutions in compiling management reports of fund-raising activity and to help them speak the same language when they compare development data with previous years and other institutions (for example, through the Council for Aid to Education's annual *Voluntary Support of Education* survey and the CASE Survey of Cumulative Campaign Activity by Educational Institutions).

On the accounting side of things, the big names are the Financial Accounting Standards Board and the American Institute of Certified Public Accountants. Both organizations deal with the broader accounting world, but with respect to nonprofits, FASB and AICPA set special standards of professional practice for accounting for gifts and presenting financial reports.

Always in the background is the Internal Revenue Service, whose policies and decisions form the legal basis for CASE and FASB guidelines (as well as for gift substantiation requirements that are separate from gift reporting standards).

It all seems so simple, doesn't it? The main federal tax agency sets guidelines, which appropriate professional associations then use to develop standards of professional practice. If a tax guideline is a tax guideline and a gift is a gift according to the IRS, what could possibly cause confusion between what development and accounting report to their constituents?

In a word: plenty!

> *Ask any fund raisers—whether they're assigned to the annual fund, major gifts, planned gifts, a capital campaign, or grant seeking—what their No. 1 responsibility is, and they will probably answer, "To raise money."*

PRINCIPLE NO. 2: ADVANCEMENT SERVICES SUPPORTS BOTH DEVELOPMENT AND ACCOUNTING (BUT FOR DIFFERENT REASONS).

Ask any fund raisers—whether they're assigned to the annual fund, major gifts, planned gifts, a capital campaign, or grant seeking—what their No. 1 responsibility is, and they will probably answer, "To raise money." Sure, other things, such as volunteer management and board development, may come into play. But these are merely a means to an end, the end being to exceed last year's gift total and meet this year's goal. Your colleagues are primarily concerned with their program's average gift amount, year-to-date comparisons, participation rates by segment, etc. They focus on gifts to their particular program within the institution.

Ask members of your accounting department why they're around and they're likely to respond, "To provide information that management can use to plan and control the budget as well as make strategic financial decisions." Sure, there are a number of varied functions within the accounting area, such as purchasing, accounts receivable, and accounts payable, all of which may be broken down by school, college, or division. But the information resulting from all of these day-to-day activities is ultimately used by senior management—as well as your auditors—to make statements and decisions about your institution's overall financial health.

What is the role of advancement services in all this? Common sense dictates that it's to provide valid and reliable financial information to both fund raisers and accounting staff so they can each perform their roles. The problem is, serving both worlds can be tricky given the differing standards development and accounting use to classify gift-related financial data.

PRINCIPLE NO. 3: WE LOOK FOR DIFFERENT THINGS AND HAVE DIFFERENT PRIORITIES.

The advancement service most closely linked to the accounting function is gift processing, in which contributions received are credited to donor records. As contributions come in, members of the advancement services staff update donor names, addresses, and marital status. Then they credit the gifts to the appropriate fund-raising program and send them to accounting to deposit in the appropriate fund or account, depending on the donor's purpose. The gift-processing staff also collects and enters into the donor's record other information, such as the gift source (individual, corporation, foundation, etc., including "recognition credit" vs. "legal credit"); whether it is a pledge payment; the date the gift came in; and its cause (that is, which mailing or phone solicitation spurred it).

Development uses this information to generate tax receipts

for donors and to compile reports that fellow advancement staff analyze to monitor success, implement strategic program changes during the current year, and plan programs for the following year. Although the variables are many and the analysis is complex, they're essential in order to plan and implement an effective fund-raising program.

It's true that members of the business and accounting staff provide data for effective budgetary planning. But they could not care less about much of the information that gift processing collects. Business and accounting are mostly concerned with gifts as revenue and how expenses are offset as a result. The term "bottom line" is very appropriate here, as most accounting reports have a single gifts entry that lists the sum total of all gifts deposited into a particular fund or account. In many ways, recognizing this difference in perspective helps to explain the blank stare you get when your business manager says year-to-date gifts are down and you respond, "Yes, but parent and alumni participation are both up 25 percent!"

PRINCIPLE NO. 4: WE TALK ABOUT THE SAME THINGS BUT VIEW THEM DIFFERENTLY.

One of the intriguing things about listening to development and accounting folks talk about each other's data is how frequently we use identical terms in obviously different ways. Many of these discussions center on the concepts of restricted, unrestricted, annual giving, and annual fund.

It's useful to see examples of this at work. Here are instructions as supplied by CASE in the annual giving section of *CASE Management Reporting Standards:*

"**Unrestricted:** Report the total outright gifts, *including realized bequests,* given by donors without any restriction, regardless of any subsequent designation by the institution to be used for current operations, to function as endowment, to construct facilities, or for other purposes. In cases where the donor expresses a preference for the gift's use but leaves the decision to the institution, report the gift as unrestricted.

"**Restricted:** Report the total outright gifts to current operations that have been restricted by the donor for academic divisions, athletics, faculty and staff compensation, research, public service and extension, library, operation and maintenance of physical plant, student financial aid, and (all) other restricted purposes."

Pretty clear, right? Now consider the FASB definitions as paraphrased from the Statement of Financial Accounting Standards No. 116:

Unrestricted support: Revenues or gains from contributions that are not restricted by donors.

Restricted support: Donor-restricted revenues or gains from contributions that increase either temporarily restricted net assets or permanently restricted net assets.

However, the FASB guideline additionally states: "Contributions with donor-imposed restrictions shall be reported as restricted support; however, donor-restricted contributions whose restrictions are met in the same reporting period may be reported as unrestricted support provided that an organization reports consistently from period to period and discloses its accounting policy."

Taken together, what does it all mean? Well, it would appear that both accounting and development share common definitions of both unrestricted and restricted, but that accounting has the flexibility to deposit and report a restricted gift as unrestricted if the donor's restriction is met during the fiscal year in which it was given.

For example, assume that your institution received several gifts for your athletic program. Following CASE standards, these gifts would be classified as restricted. On the accounting reports, however, these same gifts could be classified as unrestricted if it's deemed that they will be entirely spent according to their donor-intended purpose during the fiscal year in which they were given.

The downside to all this is the potential for reporting discrepancies between development and accounting—a potential that becomes even greater as the difference in reporting restricted gifts is multiplied across the many restricted donor purposes the CASE standards track (i.e., academic divisions, athletics, faculty and staff compensation, research, public service and extension, library, operation and maintenance of physical plant, student financial aid, and (all) other restricted purposes). The upside, however, is that both the accounting standards and the CASE standards report total gifts to current year operations, not just unrestricted or restricted gifts, which should help the many development offices responsible for the annual giving.

PRINCIPLE NO. 5: WE CAN USE OUR DIFFERENCES TO LEARN FROM EACH OTHER.

Long have we heard discussions centered on defining "annual giving" and "annual fund." From what I've seen posted on listservs and shared by various nonprofit organizations, these definitions can be roughly worded as follows:

Annual giving: (a) As defined by the individual institution, the yearly act of providing either a restricted or unrestricted gift to the institution, usually in response to an organized appeal; or (b) as a synonym for annual fund.

Annual fund: An annually occurring fund-raising program seeking and resulting in unrestricted gifts to the organization for current-year operations.

Each year, annual fund officers across the country suffer panic attacks as donors respond to appeals with gifts that are considered restricted in development circles. They debate the wisdom of giving donors the option to designate their gifts because of the pressure that results when unrestricted numbers are down (although, as described above, they may be up on the accounting side).

What your colleagues—and perhaps their senior administrators—fail to realize is that their preoccupation with restricted and unrestricted is misguided in light of the institution's accounting office reports that have a more inclusive approach (as determined by FASB et al.) to evaluating support for current-year operations. This approach is also mirrored by CAE's annual VSE survey, which is based on the *CASE Management Reporting Standards* and sponsored by CASE and the National Association of Independent Schools.

The VSE survey's taxonomy is based on the reporting standards that CASE has set. As part of comparing institutions' giving programs, both restricted and unrestricted gifts appear under the "Support for Current Operations"category. As such, restricted gifts are just as important as unrestricted in that both feed into that all-important operating support.

Recognizing this could help relieve pressure on annual fund staff as the focus shifts from annual fund gifts that are exclusively unrestricted to an annual giving program with broader appeal that seeks both restricted and unrestricted support.

While development and accounting have an obvious relationship by virtue of our overlapping involvement with contributions, the relationship can remain healthy only if we encourage ongoing communication. There are many more examples in which the development and accounting functions converge and diverge, including our respective approaches to reporting capital gifts, contributed services, planned gifts, and more. If we are to continue working together for the benefit of our greater organization, we need to continue to strive to understand and respect each other and our roles.

Perhaps even more important, we need to understand the "language" we use when "you say potAto, I say potAHto" and "you say tomAto, I say tomAHto." The last thing we want to do is call the whole relationship off.

References

AICPA Audit and Accounting Guide: Not-for-Profit Organizations. New York, NY: American Institute of Certified Public Accountants, 1997.

Carey, John L. and K. Fred Skousen. *Getting Acquainted with Accounting.* Boston, MA: Houghton Mifflin Company, 1977. 170 pages.

CASE Management Reporting Standards: Standards for Annual Giving and Campaigns in Educational Fund Raising. Washington, DC: CASE, 1996.

Morgan, David R. *Voluntary Support of Education.* New York, NY: Council for Aid to Education. Co-sponsored by CASE and the National Association of Independent Schools. Published annually.

Statement of Financial Accounting Standards No. 116: Accounting for Contributions Received and Contributions Made. Norwalk, CT: Financial Accounting Standards Board, 1993.

Chapter 21

Constructing a Productive Advancement Services Team

■ By Lynne Becker
   Assistant Vice President for Development Services
   University of Washington, and
■ Gail Ferris
   Executive Director, Alumni/Development Records
   The George Washington University

Many factors, both internal and external to advancement services, play critical roles in determining whether your operation meets its goals. These factors include budget, availability of skilled staff, your advancement function's leadership, the status of your institution's fund-raising efforts, organizational history, duties outside the advancement sphere, and many others.

Nevertheless, your operation can either overcome its limitations or fall short of its potential on the basis of one thing: teamwork. An environment that encourages teamwork is perhaps the strongest determinant of a successful advancement services office. Creating a productive team is challenging yet rewarding. To help you understand the dynamics, you need to understand the mechanics of setting up a team, the roles its members play, and the stages you're likely to encounter along the way to meeting your advancement services goals.

FORMING A TEAM

What is a team, and what can it do?

At the most basic level, a team exists when individuals work together toward a common goal.

From this short sentence, three crucial themes emerge. First, the team must work together as a unit. Second, the unit must have clear goals so its members can focus their efforts. Finally, every member must share the goals, for without universal buy-in, it's impossible to get optimal results.

Teamwork produces benefits at many levels. The organization profits from better use of staff resources because a team produces much more than people working separately. Likewise, individuals benefit from a greater sense that they're working toward a common mission.

It's helpful to recognize that teams can exist on several levels. The simplest type comes together on an ad hoc basis to solve a particular problem or work on a project of fixed duration; for example, perhaps you create a team to establish a new gift acknowledgment policy or to head off Year 2000 computer problems. Different in nature, but still governed by the same rules, are teams created within work units in advancement services—the prospect research staff, say.

Intermediate levels would involve cross-functional teams that draw on many areas of advancement services. For instance, you might have one team to address policies and procedures for a new database management system; its members would have complementary expertise but come from all of advancement services.

At the highest level of complexity are large units within still larger units, such as advancement services as a whole within the institutional advancement division and advancement within your entire campus. A World Wide Web advisory committee or integrated marketing team would be examples of teams with these complex units.

The mechanics of team building

Whether you're putting together a short-term group or molding a large standing work unit like the ones listed in the sidebar found on this page, the steps involved in team building remain fundamentally the same.

1. **Establish your team's mission.** Although a team leader should guide this exercise, all members should contribute to formulating the mission because it helps develop a sense of buy-in.

2. **Choose team members.** Six to eight is an ideal number, although teams as large as 20 can be very effective. By choosing people who already have a vested interest in the project's mission, you help to ensure that the right information is available, that decisions don't have to be revisited by those not present, and that individuals who are actually affected by the outcomes have influence. If after assembling a team you realize you overlooked someone who's important to the mission, you can always add more people.

Examine the qualifications and backgrounds of all proposed members to ascertain special contributions they can make. Valuable attributes include organizational skills; the ability to synthesize, summarize, or see the bigger picture; attention to detail; inclusiveness; and being an effective educator.

Clarifying Advancement Services Function

To create a well-running team, it's helpful to start by defining the sphere of advancement services in a rational way. Possible functions can include any number of the following:

- gift accounting,
- prospect research,
- biographical records maintenance,
- donor relations,
- reporting,
- budget,
- personnel,
- facilities and equipment,
- travel,
- supplies,
- office management, and
- mailing services.

How you assemble these functions will determine whether teams have a logical mandate within your institution. Some possible groupings include:

- administration (budget, personnel, facilities and equipment, travel, supplies, office management, mailing services);
- fiscal operations (gift accounting, budget, personnel, donor relations);
- advancement records (gift accounting, biographical records, prospect research, donor relations); and
- information services (biographical records, reporting, computer equipment)

There is no hard-and-fast rule on the best way to integrate advancement functions within the advancement services organizational structure, although the four categories listed above are emerging as some of the most common. Note, however, that you could place many of the functions in more than one group; in fact, several of them could make up a function all their own. The best grouping for you will be influenced by the factors we discussed at the start of this chapter: budget, availability of skilled staff, leadership of the advancement function, status of the institution's fund-raising efforts, organizational history, and staff duties outside the advancement sphere.

Understanding the team's makeup is essential to facilitating its success. In a later section on the leader's role, we'll discuss how the leader can observe team members to discern some of these qualities.

3. **Establish ground rules.** These are the behavioral norms team members can expect in their various interactions, especially meetings. Such rules are a powerful determinant of the group's informal structure and will heavily influence its success.

Meetings that drag on encourage spotty attendance. Enforcing time limits encourages accomplishing more in less time.

Draw up the ground rules when the team is created and see to it that everyone subscribes to them from the start, keeping in mind that you can change them later if you need to. Usually, it's the facilitator's job to monitor how well everyone adheres to the rules; we'll examine the facilitator's role in greater detail in the section on structural roles.

Areas your ground rules could cover include:
- mutual respect for all team members,
- civil behavior and good manners,
- openness to questions,
- investing in communication,
- being specific and using examples,
- dealing directly with other team members,
- understanding and valuing each others' differences,
- being committed to each others' success, and
- listening to each other.

Georgetown University's Office of Alumni and University Relations has developed a set of ground rules with a slightly different spin. Members of its team are expected to be:
- committed to the institution,
- trustworthy,
- collaborative,
- dedicated to distributed decision-making,
- innovative and risk-taking, and
- results-oriented.

Making it clear that you expect everyone to obey the ground rules relieves you or anyone else from being the "bad guy" when team members need to be reined in. In that way, ground rules guide the team's operation.

4. **Define operating procedures.** Meetings are perhaps the most important means of team communication. They provide a forum for everyone to hear the same message, air differences on matters of importance to achieving goals, and reach consensus on actions the team will take. Establishing procedures early on will reduce the amount of time you need to identify who's responsible for what as work begins. The team should start developing these operating procedures by looking at the following logistical issues that must be addressed at the outset:

- How often will the team meet?
- When will it meet?
- Where will it meet?
- How long will the meetings last?
- Who will be responsible for which of the team's tasks?

All teams must consider these same basic logistics. The ideal meeting lasts an hour to an hour and a half; busy team members usually find it impossible to set aside more time than that. Meetings that drag on encourage spotty attendance. Enforcing time limits encourages accomplishing more in less time.

The meeting room's physical layout is important. Considerations include:

- proper table configuration—one that lets all members see each other (for example, arrange the tables in an open rectangle so that members can easily see a flip chart and the person at the open end who's writing on the chart);
- comfortable chairs;
- adequate lighting;
- appropriate room temperature;
- meeting supplies, including a flip chart, tape, and markers; and
- a clock.

UNDERSTANDING TEAM ROLES AND CONCERNS

Some functions must be dealt with by the team as a whole. Team responsibilities include setting the agenda, obtaining information the group needs, taking minutes and recording other information, making decisions, and communicating with others outside the group about issues the team is addressing.

But two other kinds of functions require specific people to take the following roles.

1. Structural roles

These roles require knowledge about group process. The job of those who play structural roles is to keep a team on track and moving toward the goal. They provide guidance either about the members' roles and how they carry out their responsibilities, or about the mechanics of how a team functions best.

To fill structural roles, you need two individuals with unique responsibilities and traits: a leader and a facilitator.

- **The leader's** job is to guide the team in performing its duties. In addition to ensuring that the team meets its goals, he or she acts as a content resource for the team and knows about problem-solving techniques. The leader needs to be trained in group process, if possible, and must have strong knowledge of the team's mission and goals.

When the team comes together, the leader needs to observe closely the membership's makeup. Who are the high and low participators? Who's most influential, and how do they do the influencing? Are the majority of the members autocratic, telling others what must happen, or are they more democratic, letting others contribute their thoughts? Given the ground rules, what are the dynamics of decision-making for the group?

The leader needs to encourage behavior that contributes to creating a team atmosphere, maintaining harmonious working relationships, and getting the job done.

In addition, the leader needs to encourage behavior that contributes to creating a team atmosphere, maintaining harmonious working relationships, and getting the job done. Understanding what hinders or helps is critical to the leader's most important function: to ensure that everyone focuses on the task at hand and meets the team's goals.

- **The facilitator** is a person who understands how to make groups work well. His or her background includes education in group process, role definition, conflict resolution, meeting management, leadership issues and styles, motivation theory, decision-making styles, and similar topics.

Often, a facilitator will actually have a contract with the team. To be effective, this person must remain a neutral observer. At no time should he or she offer an opinion about substantive matters before the team. The facilitator's role is to see that team members stay within the ground rules and set operating procedures; to advise them and teach them tools and techniques that will enhance how they function; and to consult with the team leader.

2. Functional/behavioral roles

These roles focus on how team members carry out their responsibilities. The roles evolve naturally, depending on how the group processes information and solves problems. One person may assume different roles based on the nature of the task. And the roles may shift mid-task. These shifts typically occur informally as time goes by and the mission attains clarity.

Whenever people gather in a group, issues of trust inevitably arise. If you want to encourage risk taking, trust is essential. So, early in the life of your team, members should place their trust in certain other members you might call "**information resource members**." Their role will be to obtain information for the team, clarify obscure points, and summarize their findings for the rest of the team. The trust placed in them is significant because they will be, in many ways, defining the reality in which the team functions. These "I'll go and find out" roles will help the team to coalesce and get the information it needs to move forward.

Because the team will naturally seek stability, maintenance roles soon follow. Those in maintenance roles are "**helpful members**" who encourage, harmonize, effect compromise, and bring the team to consensus. These "anything is possible" team members will help the group concentrate on the bigger picture, eventually leaving worries about consensus building behind. Helpful members will facilitate movement toward the goal.

Some team members will inevitably assume blocking roles until everyone in the group feels secure. These "**obstructionists**" hold themselves out as experts on the team's business; they tend to dominate, attack, doubt, withdraw, and seek recognition. The team leader must deal with these "it will never work," know-it-all members in due course to accomplish the team's goals. Although frustrating and seemingly unproductive, spending time dealing with the issues obstructionists raise is perfectly normal, especially at the beginning. As the team matures, you'll need less and less time for this.

Typical team concerns

Just as it's common for team members to need to play several types of roles, the team will have to deal with several common types of concerns. Here are a few, as well as ideas on how to deal with them.

The team leader should not allow conflict over control to go on too long or it will slow the team down.

- **Concerns about inclusion.** All team members naturally want to feel accepted, like insiders. They want to know that they're working for a clear and worthwhile common purpose; that they receive recognition and support; and that they can draw from the background, skills, and talents of other team members. Completing activities as an entire team will foster this sense of inclusion. So will establishing ground rules, objectives, and operating procedures, and tackling behavioral issues. Once team members become "we" rather than "you," emotional maturity develops and the team can move on to bigger concerns.

- **Concerns about control.** These usually arise while a team is getting organized. Individual team members may become overzealous as a means to express their individuality or to resist group formation. They may argue among themselves and become competitive or defensive. During this period, you can expect tension, disunity, discomfort, and even open hostility. You can also expect the group to make only a small amount of progress until it organizes itself.

Remember that this self-oriented behavior is normal and frequent while the team is preparing itself to go in the right direction. In fact, this behavior is helpful in settling control and inclusion issues, which is why the team leader must be prepared to ride out the conflicts and resist imposing a solution. Such attempts would likely be fruitless anyway, as initial conflict is often a very necessary ingredient of team success.

A word of caution, however: The team leader should not allow conflict over control to go on too long or it will slow the team down. When differences persist, talk openly about conflict as a concept. The goal is to help all members of the team understand that healthy conflict is necessary for good decisions and then to manage the disagreements that arise.

- **Concerns about openness.** Emotional reactions are neither bad nor good; they're simply to be expected. However, the team's ability to encourage openness, including emotional openness, is vital. The job of the facilitator and the leader is to channel this emotional openness into a constructive relationship for the benefit of the team. If all goes well, expressing feelings freely will clear obstacles between the team and its goals.

For example, those inclined to fight are often the initiators, the critics, and the evaluators. Those inclined to gloss over troubles may reduce tension with humor, or help the group rise above petty personal issues. Each individual brings strengths to the group. You just have to manage them in an open, trusting environment.

Stages of team development

Teams tend to go through predictable stages of growth and regression. Understanding how individuals behave in groups, and knowing that this behavior is part of the dynamics of group development, will help the team develop successfully.

Several models of group development are available in the literature. In his classic article, "Developmental Sequence in Small Groups," B.W. Tuckman identified four stages in decision-making groups this way:

Stage 1: Form—This period is characterized by testing and dependence as the group gets oriented and everyone strives to feel included.

Stage 2: Storm—Intra-team conflict occurs as group members compete and try to gain control.

Stage 3: Norm—Team cohesion develops through communication and openness.

Stage 4: Perform—As team members merge their roles with their function within the group, the result is freedom and success.

Several factors determine whether the team will meet its potential. One is the extent to which the team works hard in the beginning to settle the issues that concern its members. Another is the team's willingness to recognize its progress through these stages.

Because the Form, Storm, and Norm stages result in minimal output, it's tempting to try to rush through these and hope the team achieves peak productivity. Although appealing, this idea is dysfunctional. Just as individuals go through predictable stages of growth depending on their age, experience, and maturity, teams must work through predictable stages. If members fail to deal with their problems early on, those troubles will haunt them later.

Team development can stall. Like individuals, some teams never fully function. One way to help reduce the time it takes to become fully productive while minimizing the tension and fear that are common in the Form and Storm stages is to share rumors, concerns, and expectations about the team. By promising each other there will be no surprises, team members can achieve an atmosphere of trust (the Norm stage) earlier and set aside interpersonal issues in favor of freeing the team to move on and perform.

Parting advice

Whether you're about to establish a new team or simply invigorate one you already have, keep in mind these final principles that will help the group be as effective as possible.

- **Always keep in mind the basics of teamwork.** All teams need to encourage clear and widely accepted goals and methods, a sense of inclusion, a shared interest in preserving the team, and personal satisfaction. The work must be related to something that is vital to all members and involves them in it. Each member must be able to achieve some "reward" in return for the "cost" of involvement.

- **Don't be too alarmed if being in a team stirs emotions at times.** Involvement is almost impossible without provoking some of the emotions we've described previously. In productive team efforts, however, you can use emotions constructively to meet your goals if you encourage people to share their thoughts and feelings. This provides the necessary base for the trust and vigor you need to advance team goals to fruition.

- **Don't overlook the role of rituals and ceremonies.** These bring people together and create common experiences upon which you can build trust. Celebrating milestones— work-related and not, including birthdays, promotions, and beginnings and endings—contributes to open communication and mutual trust. Relaxing together, laughing, showing appreciation, and recognizing contributions to the group's efforts are additional ways to build camaraderie.

- **And finally, remember:** If you want to increase your authority, give it away—to a team.

References

Argyris, Chris. "Teaching Smart People How to Learn," *Harvard Business Review,* Reprint No. 91301 (May-June 1991).

Bennis, Warren. *On Becoming a Leader.* Menlo Park: Addison Wesley, 1989.

Covey, Stephen R. *The Seven Habits of Highly Effective People.* New York: Simon & Schuster, 1989.

Doyle, Michael and David Strauss. *How to Make Meetings Work.* New York: Jove Books, 1982.

Fisher, Bob, and Bo Thomas. *Real Dream Teams.* Delray Beach: St. Lucie Press, 1996.

Harvey, Jerry B. "The Abilene Paradox: The Management of Agreement," *Organizational Dynamics.* Periodicals Division, American Management Association, 1988.

Scholtes, Peter R. *The Team Handbook: How to Improve Quality with Teams.* Madison, WI: Joiner Associates Inc., 1988.

Tuckman, B.W., "Developmental Sequence in Small Groups," *Psychological Bulletin,* 1965, P.63, 384-399.

Wellins, Richard, and Jill George. "The Key to Self-Directed Teams," *Training and Development Journal.* (April 1991).

Glossary

A

ACCOUNTABILITY: The recipient organization's responsibility to keep a donor informed about how it uses the donor's gift.

ACCOUNTING POLICY: A policy made by a gift-supported organization that specifies which types of gifts will be counted toward a campaign goal and which types will be excluded.

ACKNOWLEDGMENT FORM: An impersonal printed card used to acknowledge relatively small gifts. (See receipt.)

ACKNOWLEDGMENT LETTER: A letter sent by the recipient organization, or on its behalf, to the donor to express appreciation for a gift and identify how it will be used. An acknowledgment may be a form letter but is usually personalized. (See receipt.)

ACQUISITION MAILING: A mailing sent to prospects to attract new members or donors.

ACTUAL VALUE: The price that property commands when sold on the open market.

ADVANCE GIFTS: Gifts solicited and given (or pledged) in advance of a campaign's public announcement. Such gifts are necessary to give a campaign momentum and show the organizers the likelihood of success or failure. (See campaign.)

ADVANCEMENT: A term used to define the total process of advancing the mission, goals, and objectives of an organization or institution. The process includes development, public relations, and (in educational institutions) alumni or alumnae affairs. (See development.)

ADVANCEMENT SERVICES: A specialty that addresses the "back office" aspects of advancement, such as computer systems, gift regulations and compliance, policies, and procedures. (See support services.)

AICPA: The acronym of the American Institute of Certified Public Accountants, a national professional organization for CPAs. Its mission is to provide members with the resources, information, and leadership to provide services in a professional manner for the benefit of the public, employers, and clients. It is based in New York City.

ALUMNI/ALUMNAE AFFAIRS/RELATIONS: In an educational institution, the advancement area responsible for serving as a liaison between the institution and its former students and for promoting the institution to that constituency.

ANNUAL FUND: An annually occurring fundraising program that seeks unrestricted gifts for current-year operations.

ANNUAL GIVING: The yearly act of providing either a restricted or unrestricted gift to the institution, usually in response to an organized appeal. Synonym: annual fund.

ANNUAL REPORT: A yearly account of financial and organizational conditions prepared by the management of an organization.

APPRAISAL: Valuation of a gift by an external source. An appraisal is usually arranged by a donor who's claiming charitable income tax deductions for gifts-in-kind (other than gifts of stock traded on a national exchange) if the total of such gifts is over $500. If the total of such gifts exceeds $5,000 ($10,000 for gifts of closely held stock), the donor should obtain a qualified appraisal with a summary on IRS Forms 8283. (See valuation.)

APPRECIATED SECURITIES GIFT: A gift of securities with a market value greater than the donor's cost or basis. The increase in value generally represents a potential capital gain, which will incur capital gains taxes unless the property is given to a charitable organization. The value of such a gift is established by calculating the mean between the high and low prices on the date it is transferred to the organization.

APPRECIATION: (1) The increase in property's market value over its original cost or tax basis; (2) gratitude for a gift.

APRA: The acronym for the Association for Professional Researchers in Advancement, formerly the Association of Professional Researchers in America. Based in Westmont, Illinois, it's an organization to foster professional development and promote standards that enhance the expertise and status of development research and information service professionals worldwide.

AUTOMATED TELEMARKETING: Use of a computerized dialing system that manages phonathon prospects on screen, either automatically (so that the technology essentially manages the prospect pool) or manually (so that it responds to the caller's determination of the pool). Organizations that use automated telemarketing do not use phonathon cards. (See phonathon card.)

AUTOMATION: A highly technical implementation that usually involves electronic hardware; automatic, as opposed to human, operation or control of a process, equipment, or a system; or the techniques and equipment used to achieve this.

B

BASIS: The purchase price of an item of property, minus depreciation allowed or allowable as a tax deduction, plus improvements.

BATCH PROCESSING: A system that takes a set (a "batch") of commands or jobs, executes them, and returns the results, all without human intervention. This is in contrast to an interactive system in which the user's commands and the computer's responses are interleaved during a single run.

BENCHMARK: A standard by which something can be measured or judged. The most useful kind of benchmark is one tailored to a user's own typical tasks.

BEQUEST: Assets of personal property such as cash, securities, or other tangible property that a donor leaves to a charity in his or her will and for which the donor's estate will receive a charitable estate tax deduction at the time of death. A testamentary gift. (See testamentary.)

BIODEMOGRAPHIC INFORMATION: Data about constituents that provide biographical or individual preferences that are useful in creating a prospect or development profile. (See donor profile and prospect profile.)

BOOK VALUE: The amount of an asset stated in a company's records, not necessarily the amount that it could bring on the open market. (See fair market value and market value.)

C

CAE: The acronym for the Council for Aid to Education, formerly the Council for Financial Aid to Education Inc. Based in New York City, it is a nonprofit national organization dedicated both to enhancing the effectiveness of corporate and other private-sector support in improving education and to helping education institutions acquire private support more effectively. (See VSE Survey.)

CAMPAIGN: An organized effort to raise funds for a nonprofit organization through solicitation by volunteers, by direct mail, by phone, or all three. (See advance gifts.)

CAPITAL CAMPAIGN: A campaign to raise substantial funds for a nonprofit organization to finance major building projects, supplement endowment funds, and meet other needs that demand extensive outlays of capital.

CAPITAL GIFT: A gift earmarked for endowment; building construction, renovation, or remodeling; equipment; or books and other non-disposable items.

CARNEGIE CLASSIFICATION OF HIGHER EDUCATION: Groupings of American colleges and universities according to their missions. As devised by the Carnegie Foundation for the Advancement of Teaching, the categories are meant primarily to improve the precision of the Foundation's research by clustering institutions with similar programs and purposes, not to establish a hierarchy among campuses.

CASE: The acronym for the Council for Advancement and Support of Education, the publisher of this book. Based in Washington, DC, it's an international association of institutional advancement officers who include alumni administrators, fund raisers, public relations managers, publications editors, and government relations officers. CASE's mission is to help these professionals advance the cause of education and enhance their institutions by bringing in support, be it in the form of money, alumni loyalty, public esteem, or new students.

CD-ROM: Compact disc read-only memory. Manufactured in the same physical format as audio compact discs, a CD-ROM is a non-volatile optical data storage medium readable by a computer with a CD-ROM drive.

CFAE: See CAE.

CHARITABLE INSTITUTION/CHARITY: Any private institution or agency that operates on a nonprofit basis for the public good and therefore is exempt from taxation (though it must pay taxes on income from any commercial operations in which it's involved).

CHARITABLE LEAD TRUST: A trust that makes payments, either a fixed amount (annuity trust) or a percentage of trust principal (unitrust), to a charity during its term. At the end of the trust term, the principal of the trust can either go back to the donor or to heirs named by the donor. (See planned gift.)

CHARITABLE REMAINDER TRUST: A trust that makes payments, either a fixed amount (annuity trust) or a percentage of trust principal (unitrust), to whomever the donor chooses to receive income. (See planned gift.)

CID: Constituent identification number.

CLOSELY HELD STOCK: privately owned corporate stock that is not publicly traded on an exchange or in the over-the-counter market. (See securities.)

COD: Computer-originated document, a feature that comes with a document-imaging system. (See document imaging.)

COMPREHENSIVE CAMPAIGN: A campaign in which all funds, whether designated for unrestricted, restricted, capital, or endowed purposes, are counted toward the goal.

CONSTITUENCY: A category of donors and prospective donors. A constituency could be made up of alumni, parents, members, staff members, or, in a broader sense, individuals, corporations, or foundations.

CONTACT REPORT/CALL REPORT: A document filed after any contact with a prospect that outlines the content of the visit or phone call and indicates appropriate follow-up.

CONVERSION: Changing computer programs and data from one language or software system to another.

CORPORATE FOUNDATION: The philanthropic organization established to coordinate, over a period of time, the philanthropic interests of a corporation. Such a foundation can be very specific about its field of interest, often limiting grants to causes related to corporate profits. (See private foundation.)

COST BASIS: The value of an item based on its original cost.

COST/BENEFIT ANALYSIS: A financial determination of a program's effectiveness in terms of expenses incurred to produce revenue. In its simplest form, this is sometimes referred to as cost per dollar raised.

CULTIVATION: The process of exposing prospective donors to institutional activities, people, needs, and plans to the point where they're interested enough to be considered ready to give at acceptable levels.

D

DATABASE: A collection of information kept in one place and accessible by many users through the same server. A database is one component of a database management system.

DATABASE INTEGRITY: How complete, and thus reliable, information in a database is. (See data cleanup.)

DATA CLEANUP: Removal and/or compression of information in a database to improve its reliability and integrity. (See database integrity.)

DECENTRALIZED DEVELOPMENT OFFICE: A fund-raising department with staff members who are physically located throughout an institution (for example, in undergraduate and graduate schools) rather than in one main office.

DEFERRED GIFT: A donation that is arranged now and fulfilled later, usually a planned gift. An example would be when donors leave a provision in their wills to make a bequest to a charitable organization. (See planned gift.)

DEFERRED GIVING: Methods of donating that require nonprofits to wait a year or more before being able to use the gift assets. Deferred giving is now generally considered to be only part of planned giving. (See planned gift.)

DESKTOP: A personal computer designed for use on a desk or table. (See laptop.)

DEVELOPMENT: A term used to define the total process of organizational or institutional fund raising. (See advancement).

DEVELOPMENT/ADVANCEMENT PROFILE: See profile.

DIRECT MAIL CAMPAIGN: A fund drive conducted by mail, often for annual giving purposes. Such campaigns are frequently broad-based, with several mailings going out over a specified period. (See segmentation.)

DOCUMENT IMAGING: Storing records or graphic images in an electronic format. (See COD.)

DONOR PROFILE: A description of basic information about an individual contributor that's based on research and personally provided information. (See biodemographic information and prospect profile.)

DONOR RECOGNITION: The policy and practice of thanking contributors for gifts, first through immediate acknowledgment by card or letter and subsequently through personalized notes, personal expressions of appreciation directly to donors, published lists of contributors, and other appropriate ways.

DONOR RELATIONS: An area of development that works with both contributors and prospects and oversees cultivation, recognition, and stewardship.

DTC ACCOUNT: An account with the Depository Trust Co., a clearinghouse for electronic transactions of securities.

E

EDUCAUSE: An association formed from the merger of CAUSE and Educom to encourage the introduction, use, and management of information resources and technologies in teaching, learning, scholarship, research, and institutional management. It's based in Washington DC, and Boulder, CO.

ELECTRONIC SCREENING: A computer process used to determine the giving potential of a wide range of prospective donors. The process, which helps identify top prospects who are loyal and have a propensity to give, provides prospect management and tracking guidance for your development staff. The research is done in online databases and on the Internet. (See prospect screening.)

E-MAIL: Short for electronic mail. These are messages automatically passed from one computer user to another, often through computer networks and/or via modems over telephone lines.

E-MAIL DISCUSSION LISTS: Arenas on the Internet that provide subscribers with the opportunity to informally post questions and answers about a specific subject. Such lists are also known as listservs.

ENDOWMENT: Funds that are kept intact and invested. The earnings or a portion thereof are applied to purposes the donor designates.

F

FAIR MARKET VALUE: The amount for which an item or property can be sold in the marketplace. (See book value and market value.)

FASB: The acronym of the Financial Accounting Standards Board of the Financial Accounting Foundation. Based in Norwalk, Connecticut, FASB sets the standards for financial accounting and reporting for nonprofits as well as the business world. The standards are used by corporations, charities, and other organizations that issue financial statements; by auditors; and by users of financial information.

FIELD: An area on a data record in which specific information about a constituent is located. Examples of fields include first name, salutation, and type of gift.

FILE MANAGEMENT: A method used to organize records, either on a database or in a physical location.

FUND ACCOUNT: A category for each type of restriction. Organizations keep such categories separate in order to keep track of a donor's wishes; accounts are later grouped for presentation in the financial statements.

G

GIFT: A voluntary transfer of things of value, usually in the form of cash, checks, securities, real property, or personal property. Gifts may come from individuals, industry, foundations, and other sources; recipients can use them for unrestricted or restricted purposes. Charities make no commitment of resources or services in return for gifts, other than possibly agreeing to put the gift to use as the donor designates. (See personal property and securities.)

GIFT ANNUITY: A contract between a nonprofit and a donor in which, in return for a donation of cash or other assets, the organization agrees to pay the donor or the donor's designee a fixed payment for life, for which the donor can also claim a charitable tax deduction. (See planned gift.)

GIFT-IN-KIND: A donation other than cash. (See in-kind contribution.)GIFT PROCESSING: The procedure of entering contributions into a database, thereby crediting the donor.

H

HARD-DRIVE CAPACITY: The amount of information that can be stored on a computer hard drive, one or more rigid magnetic disks rotating about a central axle with associated read/write heads and electronics.

HARDWARE: The physical, touchable, material parts of a computer or other system. The term is used to distinguish these fixed parts of a system from the more changeable software or data components that it executes, stores, or carries. (See software.)

I

IMPORT/EXPORT CAPABILITY: Ability of a software program to bring in or transmit data from or to other programs.

INDEPENDENT AUXILIARY: A company that is a subsidiary of another company but has its own executive officers.

INFRASTRUCTURE: Basic support services for computing, particularly national networks.

IN-HONOR-OF GIFT: A donation that's generally a tribute to a living individual and occasionally designated by the donor for a specific purpose. (See memorial gift.)

IN-KIND CONTRIBUTION: A gift of equipment, supplies, or other property instead of money. The donor may place a monetary value on the gift for tax purposes. (See appraisal, gift-in-kind, and valuation.)

INTEGRATED SOFTWARE: A computer program that offers components that can be used in tandem with other programs.

INTERFACE: A boundary across which two systems communicate; a hardware connector used to link to other devices or a convention used to allow communication between two software systems.

INTERNET: The vast collection of interconnected networks that all use the TCP/IP protocols and t

hat evolved from the ARPANET of the late 1960s and early '70s.

IRREVOCABLE: Incapable of being recalled or revoked; unchangeable; irreversible; unalterable; impossible to retract. The term usually pertains to pledges or planned gifts.

L

LAN: Local Area Network. A data communications network that is geographically limited, allowing easy interconnection of terminals, microprocessors, and computers within adjacent buildings.

LAPTOP: A portable personal computer of a size suitable to rest comfortably on one's legs as opposed to on a desktop. (See desktop.)

LEGACY: A gift of property by will, especially of money or personal property; a bequest.

LETTER OF INTENT: A statement of a prospect's intention to make a specified gift or legacy; used when a prospect prefers to avoid making a pledge. Because it could constitute a binding obligation under some circumstances, the prospective donor should seek legal counsel before executing such a letter. (See pledge.)

LIFE INCOME GIFT: See planned gift.

LYBUNT: An acronym that identifies donors who gave Last Year But Unfortunately Not This year. (See SYBUNT.)

M

MAIL CAMPAIGN: See direct mail campaign.

MAINFRAME: A term originally referring to the cabinet containing the central processor unit or "main frame" of a room-filling batch machine. The word was later applied to big iron machines after the emergence of smaller "minicomputer"

designs in the early 1970s.

MAJOR GIFT: A large gift, probably of $10,000 or greater, usually meant for capital purposes.

MARKET VALUE: As pertaining to endowment, the book value plus undistributed yield. (See book value and fair market value.)

MATCHING GIFT: An eligible contribution by an eligible corporation on behalf of an eligible employee whose eligible gift to an eligible institution starts the process.

MEMORIAL GIFT: A contribution generally commemorating a deceased individual and occasionally designated by the donor for a specific purpose. (See in-honor-of gift.)

MERGE/PURGE: A computer operation that combines two or more files of names by using a matching process to produce one file that's free of duplicates.

MIS: Management Information System. A computer system, usually based on a mainframe or minicomputer, designed to provide managers with up-to-date information on an organization's performance, such as fund-raising totals.

MISSION STATEMENT: A concise description of the purpose of an organization.

MOVES MANAGEMENT: A method of organizing donor cultivation that focuses on maintaining a strong, orderly relationship between donor and institution.

MURPHY'S LAW: If anything can go wrong, it will.

N

NACUBO: The acronym for the National Association of College and University Business Officers. It's a Washington, DC-based nonprofit professional organization representing chief administrative and financial officers at more than 2,100 colleges and universities. NACUBO's mission is to promote sound management and financial practices.

NAIS: The acronym for the National Association of Independent Schools. It's a Washington, DC-based voluntary membership organization that represents more than 1,100 private pre-collegiate schools and associations in the United States and abroad. The association speaks for member schools to national and regional media, to 10 federal agencies, and to 13 Congressional committees. On behalf of independent schools, NAIS tracks and analyzes legislation and regulations in a number of areas, including tax, environmental health hazards, and education.

NETWORK SERVER: A computer, or a software package, that provides a specific kind of service to client software running on other computers.

NIMCRUT: A planned giving term meaning net income with make-up charitable remainder unitrust.

NONPROFIT ORGANIZATION: A group that qualifies for federal income-tax exemption under Section 501(c)(3) of the Internal Revenue Code or under other 501 classifications. (See Section 501(c)(3).)

NSFRE: The acronym for the National Society of Fund Raising Executives. Based in Alexandria, Virginia, it's a professional association for individuals responsible for generating philanthropic support for a wide variety of nonprofit charitable organizations.

O

OCR: Optical Character Recognition. It's a mechanism through which a computer identifies printed or written characters.

ONLINE PROFESSIONAL DISCUSSION GROUPS: See e-mail discussion lists.

P

PARTICIPATION: Percentage of solicited constituents who make gifts. Participation is calculated by dividing the number of donors by the number of constituents solicited.

PERSONAL PROPERTY: Cash, stocks, bonds, notes, paintings, furniture, jewelry, and other similar possessions other than real estate. (See gift and securities.)

PHONATHON: A fund-raising effort in which either volunteers or paid callers solicit gifts or pledges by telephone. Employed especially in annual fund campaigns.

PHONATHON CARD: A form that provides the phone solicitor with biodemographic information and a giving history for the prospective donor. (See automated telemarketing.)

PLANNED GIFT/PLANNED GIVING: A type of charitable donation, requiring some planning, that's popular because it can provide valuable tax benefits and/or income for life. The terms often refer to the process of making a charitable gift of estate assets to one or more nonprofit organizations; a donation that requires consideration and planning in light of the donor's overall estate plan; or part of an individual's major gift strategy, generally involving a bequest or trust. (See charitable lead trust, charitable remainder trust, deferred gift, deferred giving, gift annuity, and pooled income fund.)

PLEDGE: A verbal or written commitment by a constituent to make a gift within a specific time frame. (See letter of intent.)

PLEDGE CARD: A printed form used by solicitors in seeking what is most often a legally binding commitment from a prospect.

PLEDGE REMINDER: A printed form that the charity sends on regular schedule to a constituent who has made a pledge but has not completed full payment.

POOLED INCOME FUND: A planned gift in which a charity accepts contributions from many donors into a fund, the charity keeps the principal, and the charity distributes the income from the fund to each donor or recipient of the donor's choosing. Each income recipient then receives income in proportion to his or her share of the fund, and the donor receives a charitable income tax deduction. This form of trust is described in paragraph (5) of Internal Revenue Code Subsection 642(c). (See planned gift)

PREMIUM: A tangible item or benefit that an institution gives in exchange for a contribution, such as a tie with the school logo or free tickets to attend an event. Depending on both its cost and fair market value, a premium could affect the tax deductability of the original gift. (See quid pro quo, tax deductibility.)

PRIVATE FOUNDATION: An organization established to coordinate, over a period of time, the philanthropic interests of a private entity such as an individual or family. Such a foundation can be very specific as to its field of interest, often limiting grants to causes related solely to the entity's interests. (See corporate foundation.)

PRIVATE SUPPORT: Philanthropic support from sources other than the government.

PROCESSING SPEED: The amount of time a job takes to run on a computer, given that it has exclusive and uninterrupted use of the CPU (central processing unit).

PROFILE: See donor profile and prospect profile.

PROPOSAL: A written request or application for a gift or grant that includes why the project or program is needed, who will carry it out, and how much it will cost. (See RFP.)

PROSPECT LIST: A roster of potential donors maintained by a development or campaign office.

PROSPECT MAILING: See acquisition mailing.

PROSPECT MANAGEMENT: See moves management.

PROSPECT PROFILE: A research report detailing all of the pertinent facts about a potential donor, including resources, relationships, and past giving. (See biodemographic information and donor profile.)

PROSPECT RATING: A procedure for evaluating the giving potential of various potential donors. The ratings depend on the judgments of knowledgeable people who are functioning as a special campaign committee or on assessments made on the basis of specific criteria.

PROSPECT RESEARCH: A development office's use of numerous reference sources to search for pertinent information about potential donors of all types, including ones who may not already be known to the organization. (See electronic screening.)

PROSPECT SCREENING: Identifying potential donors and assessing their ability and inclination to give through information gleaned from their peers. (See electronic screening.)

Q

QUASI-ENDOWMENT: Funds that are retained and invested and are either unrestricted or restricted. (See restricted gift and unrestricted gift.)

QUERY FUNCTION: A user's (or an agent's) request for information, generally as a formal request to a database or search engine.

QUID PRO QUO: A contribution in return for which the donor receives something back, such as a premium, which could affect the tax deductibility of the donor's gift. In the original Latin, the term means "something for something." (See tax deductibility.)

R

RAM: Random Access Memory. A data storage device for which the order of access to different locations does not affect the speed of access. This is in contrast to a magnetic disk or magnetic tape, where it is much quicker to access data sequentially because accessing a nonsequential location requires physical movement of the storage medium rather than just electronic switching.

RECEIPT: An impersonal printed form sent to the donor that confirms a gift has been received and put toward its designation. (See acknowledgment form and acknowledgment letter.)

RESEARCH: See prospect research.

RESTRICTED GIFT: A donation for a specified purpose as clearly stated by the donor, for example, for academic divisions, athletics, or research.

RFP: Request for proposal. A written notice listing the requirements for submitting an proposal for a gift or grant. (See proposal.)

S

SABBATICAL: A leave of absence from the institution, usually given to academicians, but occasionally to administrators. The leave is generally devoted to research and ultimately the production of a paper, proposal, or publication.

SECTION 501(C)(3): The section of the Internal Revenue Code under which charitable, religious, educational, scientific, literary, and other organizations that meet the requirements are exempt from federal income tax.

SECURITIES: Evidence of property, such as a bond or a certificate of stock. (See closely held stock, gift, and personal property.)

SEGMENTATION: The process of dividing a constituency into groups to personalize the solicitation material as much as possible, usually for a direct mail campaign. (See direct mail campaign.)

SOFTWARE: The instructions executed by a computer, as opposed to the physical device on which they run. (See hardware.)

SOLICITATION MAILING: See direct mail campaign.

SOURCE: Origin of the gift, such as an individual, corporation, or foundation.

STEERING COMMITTEE: A group of leaders that bears overall responsibility for establishing a campaign or development program until a permanent campaign committee assumes this responsibility.

STEWARDSHIP: A program of annual reporting to donors that tells how their gifts were used and often inspires repeat giving. (See donor relations.)

STOCK POWER: A written form giving the charitable organization the power to liquidate a gift of securities. (See securities.)

STRATEGIC PLAN/VISION: A concise written statement of an institution's future direction.

SUPPORT SERVICES: Technical areas of a development program or fund-raising campaign that deal with prospect research, mailings of appeal letters, gift processing, list preparation, clerical operations, and so on. (See advancement services.)

SYBUNT: An acronym that identifies donors who gave Some Year But Unfortunately Not This. (See LYBUNT.)

T

TAX DEDUCTIBILITY: That portion of a gift that donors can deduct from their taxes, depending on their tax bracket and whether the charitable institution provided any quid pro quo services. (See quid pro quo.)

TECHNOLOGY COMPATIBLE: The ability of different systems, such as programs, file formats, protocols, and even programming languages, to work together or exchange data.

TELETHON: See phonathon.

TESTAMENTARY: Of or pertaining to a will; bequeathed by will; done, appointed by, or founded on a testament or will. (See bequest.)

TOKEN VALUE: A nominal price placed on a gift as a matter of form. The IRS publishes token values in its final bulletin of the year—for example, for 1998 you would check IRB98-52.

U

UNRESTRICTED GIFT: A donation made unconditionally and without any restriction; the reverse of a restricted gift. (See restricted gift.)

URL: Uniform Resource Locator. It's the electronic address of an Internet location; the standard way to give the address of any resource on the Internet that is part of the World Wide Web; and a draft standard for specifying the location of an object on the Internet, such as a file or a newsgroup.

USER: Someone doing "real work" with the computer, operating it as a means rather than an end; or someone who applies a program, however skillfully, without getting into the internals of the program.

V

VALUATION: The act of estimating value or worth; setting a price; an appraisal of the value of something. (See appraisal.)

VENDOR: A seller; someone who exchanges goods or services for money.

VSE SURVEY: The Voluntary Support of Education survey published annually by the Council for Aid to Education. The survey includes detailed information on gift income, enrollment, endowment market value, and educational and general expenditures from colleges, universities, and private elementary and secondary schools. The figures are on private gifts and grants received from alumni, parents, other individuals, foundations, corporations, and other organizations. (See CAE.)

W

WORM: Write Once, Read Many. The term applies to optical disks.

Y

YEAR 2000 COMPLIANT: Computer programs that can accept, store, calculate, and print 21st-century dates as well as 20th-century dates. That is, they have the ability to identify January 1, 2000, as occurring after December 31, 1999.